FUNCTIONAL
BEHAVIORAL
ASSESSMENT

FUNCTIONAL BEHAVIORAL ASSESSMENT

Mary E. McConnell, Ph.D.
Carol J. Cox, MS. Ed.
Dawn D. Thomas, Ph.D.
Perry B. Hilvitz, MS. Ed.

LOVE PUBLISHING COMPANY
Denver • London • Sydney

Published by Love Publishing Company
Denver, Colorado 80222

Copyright © 2001 Love Publishing Company
Printed in the United States of America
ISBN 0-89108-277-8
Library of Congress Catalog Card Number 00-104333

CONTENTS

FIGURES

TABLES

Introduction to IDEA and Functional Assessment

Discipline and behavior issues are becoming of increased concern in both general and special education. Teachers in our public schools are responsible for teaching students with varying disabilities who have behavioral and educational needs (Fuchs & Fuchs, 1994). Some students with special needs bring problems and behaviors to classrooms that many general education teachers are not prepared or equipped to address (Bradley & West, 1994; Kauffman & Wong, 1991; McAuley & Johnson, 1993).

Among behaviors typically exhibited by these students teachers find the following particularly challenging: attention problems, off-task behavior, difficulty with task completion, disruptions, lack of organizational skills, verbal and physical outbursts, impulsive behaviors, passive and aggressive behavior, poor social and interpersonal skills and other inappropriate behaviors. (Hallahan & Kauffman, 1994; Zaragoza, Vaughn, & McIntosh, 1991) Student behavior will continue to be a major focus area for educators.

To be successful in school-based settings, some students may require behavior interventions, modifications, curriculum changes, and strategies developed into a Behavior Intervention Plan that is implemented and monitored closely. Many students may be helped only through the use of a systematic individualized Behavior Intervention Plan developed through the functional assessment process.

IDEA and Functional Assessment

One of the main themes of the 1997 IDEA Amendments is the remediation of behavior and discipline problems. As a result, new demands are placed on school districts in how they discipline students with disabilities. School districts are being asked to deal with behavior problems and discipline issues proactively (Yell & Shriner, 1997) and to consider the use of positive interventions before resorting to punishment as an intervention (Gable, Quinn, Rutherford, & Howell,

1

1998). As part of this process, this law places great emphasis on conducting functional behavior assessments and writing Behavior Intervention Plans for students with disabilities who have behavioral issues that result in disciplinary action. The mandate requirement represents a strong attempt to improve educational opportunities for students with disabilities. As Behavior Intervention Plans are designed, they help to promote and ensure the continued educational services to these students (FAPE).

Many educators are not familiar with the assessment-intervention process and find the functional assessment process unclear, cumbersome, and too clinical. Additionally, there are many questions from educators on how to complete this process. That is why we felt the need to develop a user-friendly guide to help school-based personnel through the functional assessment process. We recognize that it is a great leap to expect traditionally trained teachers to shift from traditional management procedures to clinically based procedures that rely on analysis to predict behavior outcomes and select interventions based on the results of data collection.

As a result of this IDEA requirement, teachers will need staff development activities, training, practice, and feedback in how to conduct functional assessments and how to write effective Behavior Intervention Plans (Johns, 1998). More importantly, teachers need to have knowledge and expertise in how to implement appropriate research-based interventions that address specific behavior problems.

HELPING EDUCATORS UNDERSTAND FUNCTIONAL ASSESSMENT

Functional assessment can be overwhelming to educators who are not familiar with the process. This manual is designed specifically for persons who have limited training in applied behavior analysis and functional assessment procedures but is also a helpful tool for persons who have a background in behavior applications.

Specifically, the publication will help educators understand the purpose and meaning of the functional behavior assessment process and how to identify and assess behavior. The book shows how to develop and write effective Behavior Intervention Plans using data collected during the functional assessment, presenting many useful forms that can be used to complete the process.

The work is written for general and special educators, staff development personnel, school psychologists, counselors, administrators, and other school personnel working in school settings who are involved in the functional assessment process. Personnel who work in juvenile correctional facilities, residential treatment centers, and alternative education programs who have direct contact with students with challenging behavior will also find this publication helpful.

THE FUNCTION OF FUNCTIONAL ASSESSMENT

Currently, the term functional assessment is being widely used in both general and special education settings. For some educators and others, functional assessment is a new phenomenon and they find its meaning, purpose, and process unclear. In order to be effective in conducting functional assessments, persons involved must have a clear understanding of the term. This chapter begins by giving a clear definition of what functional assessment is and presents functional assessment as a problem-solving team process. Other topics discussed are: (a) When do you conduct a functional assessment? (b) Who should conduct the functional assessment? and (c) How long does it take?

WHAT IS FUNCTIONAL ASSESSMENT?

Functional assessment is an information-gathering and fact-finding process by which information about a student's behavior can be collected from multiple sources. It is a process for determining and understanding the cause of a student's behavior and its relationship to the environment in which it occurs. The functional assessment process seeks to understand when, where, and why the behavior occurs. The cause or purpose of a student's behavior is sometimes referred to as the "function" of the behavior (Quinn, Gable, Rutherford, Nelson, & Howell, 1998), hence the name "functional assessment."

Functional assessment of student behavior is not a new phenomenon. The process has been used widely for years by persons in the field of applied behavior analysis as a way to understand behaviors and as a method of intervention. The functional assessment process was originally designed to provide an understanding of behaviors exhibited by students who were unable to verbalize their intents (generally students with communication disorders) (O'Neil, Horner, Albin, Storey, & Sprague, 1990). Functional assessment procedures have also been used extensively with students with severe disabilities (Carr & Durand, 1985; Dunlap, Kern, dePerczel, Clark, Wilson, Childs, White, & Falk, 1993) as a way to reduce disruptive and inappropriate behavior. An understanding of the function of their behaviors increased the success of intervention plans developed to affect those behaviors.

The functional assessment process is now being used in public school settings with students with mild disabilities who demonstrate behavior problems. The term "mild disabilities" typically refers to children with learning disabilities, mild mental retardation, or behavioral disorders (Meese, 1994). Functional assessment can be used as a process by educators to help explain the causes of behavior and as a tool to implement strategies needed to redirect or alter student behaviors.

Functional assessment is a valuable tool for gathering information needed to develop effective Behavior Intervention Plans (BIPs) as it combines assessment and intervention as a way to address the behavioral issues of students. The Behavior Intervention Plan should include positive behavior interventions, strategies, and supports to address the problem behavior identified. Functional assessment uses a variety of sources and methods to determine the causes of behavior. They are:

- Direct observations of the student's behavior
- Formal and informal assessments
- Teacher/student/parent interviews (oral and written)
- Checklists
- Rating scales
- Academic probes/assessment
- Environmental and classroom variables
- School records/grades
- IEP information
- Medical information
- Prior interventions and results

FUNCTIONAL ASSESSMENT AS A PROBLEM-SOLVING TEAM PROCESS

We propose that a problem solving, team-based approach be used throughout the functional assessment process. This idea is supported by Miller, Tansy, and Hughes (1998), who believes that this approach may work better when conducting school-based functional behavior assessments. The team works together collaboratively using effective problem-solving and communication skills to complete the functional assessment and write the Behavior Intervention Plan.

As noted, conducting the functional assessment and writing the behavior intervention plan is a team process. To be effective, functional assessment teams must work together to create plans that help students to function successfully in school. Therefore, the team comes together to assess and analyze the student's behavior and then determines and selects the most appropriate interventions to be tried.

During the functional assessment team meeting the team:

1. completes the Functional Assessment Interview Form

2. reviews, analyzes and discusses the data and the information collected
3. identifies predictors of the behavior
4. develops a hypothesis statement
5. writes the Behavior Intervention Plan

The functional assessment facilitator leads the inquiry to address all information that may be related to the student's behavior.

As noted earlier, the purpose of the functional assessment is to try to understand why the problem behavior is occurring and how it relates to the student's present environment. Contextual information about the behavior such as the antecedents (events that occur prior to the behavior) of the behavior, setting events, classroom environment, and curriculum and instruction, as well as the student's functioning in other environments, is examined by the team. Specifically, factors that may be initiating or sustaining the behavior in question are discussed (Quinn et al., 1998).

Some common reasons for student behavior include:

1. Attention from peers and adults
2. Escape or avoidance from a non preferred or difficult task or situation
3. Control or power over events, people and situations

By understanding the conditions, triggers, and supporting consequences of the behavior team, members can analyze and draw conclusions about the behavior(s) in question.

It is through the team process that interventions and modifications in the instructional environment are developed and put in place in an attempt to reduce and/or extinguish the problem behavior while retaining instructional integrity in the student's educational program. Documentation of this collaborative effort is expressed in a student's Behavior Intervention Plan.

Functional assessment has been demonstrated to be a valuable process in working with students who have a variety of disabilities and in a variety of settings. It not only assists in providing valuable information to the teacher, it also provides valuable information to the student, allowing both the opportunity to constructively modify the necessary contingencies needed to bring about positive outcomes (Quinn et al., 1998). *The outcome of the functional assessment process is to produce changed behavior for students with disabilities so that they can become successful in school.*

WHEN DO YOU CONDUCT A FUNCTIONAL ASSESSMENT?

As part of the Individuals with Disabilities Education Act (IDEA) Amendments of 1997, local education agencies (LEAs) are now required to conduct a functional assessment and develop a Behavioral Intervention Plan for students with disabilities who have behavioral issues that result in a suspension or removal for more than 10 days or more in a school year. This process must be conducted either before or not later than 10 business days (school days) after:

1. first removing the child for more than 10 days in a school year and
2. commencing a removal that constitutes a change in educational placement or service

Although P L 105-17 designates that Functional Behavior Assessments must be conducted for children who exhibit behaviors that result in change of placement and removals of more than 10 days, there are other times when a functional behavior assessment should be conducted. These include the following:

1. during the prereferral intervention process;
2. during a comprehensive evaluation for students exhibiting significant behavior problems;
3. when investigating and attempting to treat common but significant academic and behavioral deficits;
4. during the reevaluation process for students with problem behaviors;
5. for Section 504 accommodation plans; and
6. for measuring the impact of any intervention strategies (e.g., pharmacological treatments).

Additionally, functional behavior assessments can provide meaningful data when evaluating a student in order to determine eligibility for special education services. Functional assessment can be used in both general and special education classrooms when a student repeatedly exhibits undesirable behavior in the classroom and when a student's problem behavior impedes his/her or another student's ability to benefit from classroom instruction.

Finally, functional assessment can be used for students for whom traditional methods of intervention and behavior management have failed and for students who are subject to school discipline. In determining when to conduct a functional assessment, simply begin the process as soon as problem behaviors are noted repeatedly.

WHO SHOULD CONDUCT THE FUNCTIONAL ASSESSMENT?

We suggest that any time the functional behavior assessment process is applied, the format of choice is the multidisciplinary team. P L 105-17 suggests that the following make up the multidisciplinary team: a general education teacher, special education teacher, parents, a person qualified to interpret test data, an administrator capable of allocating funds, and whenever appropriate, the child (Individuals with Disabilities Act of 1997). We also suggest that other caregivers in the child's life, such as the school counselor, school social worker, support facilitator, paraeducator, and applicable teachers, can serve as active participants on the team.

Miller, Tansy, and Hughes (1998) reported that multidisciplinary teams (e.g., child study teams or problem-solving teams) who followed a "multimodal approach" that focused on the integration and interpretation of data, kept members focused, on-task, goal-directed, and productive in meetings (p. 16). Shaw and Swerdik (1995) pointed out that other types of problem-solving teams without the focus on actual data analysis had difficulty staying focused, talked about irrelevant topics, and encountered problems reaching solutions.

Many districts have problem-solving teams (child study team, behavior intervention team, pre-assessment team, or student improvement team). These teams can serve as the functional assessment team or the facilitation of the functional assessment process can be channeled through the IEP team. Team members can consist of the special education teacher, general education teachers, school psychologist, behavioral analyst/specialist, social worker, school nurse, school counselor, related service personnel, parents, general education administrators, special education administrators, and other school staff. There must be a person on the team who is knowledgeable about the student. Parents should also be active participants on the team.

FUNCTIONAL ASSESSMENT FACILITATOR

Although we propose that this be a team effort, someone on the team who is knowledgeable of the functional assessment process should lead the process. This person can be identified as the functional assessment facilitator.

We suggest that at each school a person be assigned as a functional assessment facilitator. This person would oversee functional assessment procedures and processes for the school(s) to which they are assigned. In other words, they are the managers of the functional assessment process.

Qualified persons that may fit the role of the functional assessment facilitator are special education teachers, school psychologists, counselors, support facilitators, and behavioral analysts. The functional assessment facilitator should be knowledgeable and have experience and expertise in the following areas:

1. applied behavior analysis
2. data collection procedures
3. collaboration and problem solving
4. resources available in the building
5. the unique characteristics of the school environment
6. effective and positive interventions and strategies

School districts should provide additional training as necessary for the functional assessment facilitator to ensure adequate knowledge and skills and alter job assignments so that the person can fulfill this role appropriately.

Along with monitoring functional assessment procedures, the facilitator is responsible for fulfilling the following roles or for designating someone else to do so: (a) keep individual files (forms) on student, (b) select data collector(s), (c) conduct interviews with staff, student, and parent, (d) communicate with the functional assessment team members, parents, building and district administrators, and (e) identify intervention support staff who will provide assistance to the teacher who is implementing different strategies with students. In addition, the functional assessment facilitator makes sure everyone on the team understands the language used during the meeting and clarifies team member roles and responsibilities.

Although the functional assessment facilitator is the one who coordinates and oversees the entire process and makes sure it is implemented in an appropriate and timely way, other persons on the team, including the classroom teacher, can be responsible for completing and gathering specific pieces of information that comprise the functional assessment process.

THE TEACHER'S ROLE

Classroom teachers play a vital role in the functional assessment process. In cases other than school suspensions for disciplinary actions and change of educational placements, the classroom teacher (a) can initiate the process, (b) is responsible for much of the data collection, (c) serves as an active participant in the team problem-solving process, and (d) is directly involved in the implementation of the Behavioral Intervention Plan.

HOW LONG DOES IT TAKE TO CONDUCT A FUNCTIONAL ASSESSMENT?

Conducting a functional assessment is not a 30-to-45 minute process. The procedures outlined in this manual cannot be adequately completed in one day. To get a complete picture of the student's target behavior, there needs to be time to observe, assess, and analyze behavior, collect information about the student, and time for team-based collaboration and decision making. Time is also needed to select appropriate interventions, supports, and strategies.

The authors have found that functional assessments can be conducted adequately in 6 weeks. The key lies in the effectiveness of the functional assessment facilitator who has the ability to move the process along. We suggest the following timeline as a guide for conducting functional behavior assessments.

Functional Behavior Assessment Timeline

Week 1
The functional assessment facilitator meets with the classroom teacher and:

1. completes Target Behavior Assessment Form (Figure 2)
2. identifies and describes the target behavior(s)
3. selects observation measures and assessment tools
4. schedules next meeting to be held immediately following completion of baseline

Week 1 and Week 2
The classroom teacher(s) and or selected personnel:

1. collect baseline data (5 consecutive school days) (Figures 5, 6, and 7)

2. conduct interviews, gather medical, educational and environmental information, and make additional informal observations (Figures 11, 12, and 13)
3. hold scheduled team meeting
4. complete functional assessment interview form designed specifically to be completed at the team meeting (Figure 14)
5. analyze and discuss data collected
6. develop hypothesis statement (Table 2)
7. write Behavior Intervention Plan (Figure 16)
8. provide training to teachers in how to implement strategies, interventions, and modifications if necessary
9. schedule meetings for follow-ups

Weeks 3 through 5
The classroom teacher(s), selected personnel, and the functional assessment facilitator:
1. implement Behavior Intervention Plan
2. collect intervention data
3. conduct weekly follow-up meetings

Week 6
The functional assessment team led by the functional assessment facilitator:
1. conducts follow-up meeting to review intervention plan and make decisions about future treatments.

In some cases, depending on the severity of the behavior and the amount of data received, the team may find it difficult to complete all of activities that have been suggested for Weeks 1 and 2. Therefore, the team may find it necessary to schedule a second meeting. The team, led by a functional assessment facilitator, will continue to monitor the intervention plan and review and revise it as needed.

Timeline for Long-Term Suspensions

The timeline just suggested may need to be altered and modified for cases that involve long-term suspensions. For example, this would apply to students with disabilities in cases where their removal constitutes a change of placement for more than 10 days or for up to 45 days to an interim alternative educational setting that resulted from: (a) a weapon being brought to school, (b) drug offenses (Sec. 300.520) (a) (2), or (c) substantial likelihood of injury to the child or others as determined by a hearing officer (Sec. 300.521).

If the school has not conducted a functional behavior assessment and does not have a Behavior Intervention Plan for the student before the behavior that resulted in the suspension, the IEP team must convene and conduct a functional behavior assessment and write an appropriate Behavior Intervention Plan to address the behavior not later than 10 days after disciplinary action has been taken.

Due to the 10-day time factor involved, the functional assessment process must move quickly. The team meets to develop a modified assessment plan to gather information that addresses the behavior that resulted in long-term suspension. This assessment gathering process may involve:

1. Interviewing and talking to people who were directly involved in the incident or who witnessed the event.
2. Gathering information about what occurred prior to, during and immediately following the incident.
3. Interviewing the student's teachers and other students.
4. Reviewing student records to screen for similar behavior patterns.
5. Looking at other sources of information such as medical records, discipline records, grades, academic information that the team may find valuable to assist in developing a Behavior Intervention Plan.

After the functional behavior assessment has been completed, a Behavior Intervention Plan is developed to address the behavior that resulted in the suspension. The Behavior Intervention Plan is implemented in the interim alternative educational setting as well as when the student returns to his or her home school. If the child already has a Behavioral Intervention Plan, the IEP team must review the plan and modify it, as necessary, to address the behavior.

FUNCTIONAL ASSESSMENT PROCESS

Haynes (1998) identified four problem areas that may be a hindrance to the functional assessment process: the lack of procedures, poor data collection methods, disagreement in decision-making, and cost. For functional assessments to be effective, a specific procedure must be followed.

FUNCTIONAL ASSESSMENT PROCEDURE

McConnell, Hilvitz, and Cox (1998) outlined a 10-step procedure school districts can follow when conducting functional assessments in schools. The 10 steps are shown in Figure 1.

The steps described by McConnell et al. (1998) include easy-to-use data collection methods that can be used to document application of the functional assessment process in an inexpensive yet effective manner. A team consensus

---

FUNCTIONAL ASSESSMENT STEPS

1. Identify the Student's Behavior
2. Describe/Define the Problem Behavior
3. Collect Behavioral Baseline Data and Academic Information
4. Describe the Environment and Setting Demands
5. Complete the Functional Assessment Interview Form
6. Develop a Hypothesis
7. Write a Behavioral Intervention Plan
8. Implement Behavioral Intervention Plan
9. Collect Behavioral Data
10. Conduct a Follow-up Team Meeting

FIGURE 1. Functional Assessment Steps.

format is emphasized throughout the 10 steps. The first six steps, which make up the functional assessment process, are presented in this chapter. They consist of identifying, defining, and observing the problem behavior, assessing environmental factors, conducting interviews, and predicting why the behavior occurs (writing a hypothesis statement).

> Step 1. Identify the Student's Behavior
> Step 2. Describe the Problem Behavior
> Step 3. Collect Behavioral Baseline Data and Academic Information
> Step 4. Describe the Environment and Setting Demands
> Step 5. Complete the Functional Assessment Interview Form
> Step 6. Develop a Hypothesis

Using the procedure outlined in this chapter, school-based personnel will be able to collect a broad base of information about the student's target behavior (the behavior that will be addressed during the functional assessment process). The information gathered during Steps 1-5 provide valuable information that can be used in developing a hypothesis statement (Step 6) for the behavior. This in turn is used in writing the Behavior Intervention Plan.

Step 1. Identify the Student's Behavior

It is very important to identify the problem behavior of greatest concern (Kaplan & Carter, 1995). Therefore, the first step in conducting a functional assessment is to identify the problem behavior(s). This process is best accomplished by interviewing the referring teacher (at the elementary level) or the referring team (at the secondary level). The functional assessment facilitator should act as the interviewer and coordinate this step.

The authors suggest that the functional assessment process begin by listing all problem behaviors the student is exhibiting in the school setting. Next, the most overt or the most challenging behavior should be determined. Answering the questions below can facilitate this discussion:

1. How frequently does the behavior occur?
2. How intense is the behavior?
3. How long does the behavior last?
4. Who does the behavior affect?
5. Where does the behavior occur?
6. When is the behavior least likely to occur?
7. What are the results of the behavior?
8. With whom does the behavior occur?
9. Does the behavior vary significantly from the behavior of other students in the class?
10. Which problem behavior, if alleviated, could predictably bring about a much greater level of success for the student?

By gathering answers to these questions, team members can draw conclusions about problem behaviors and select the most overt behavior(s) with the greatest impact on the student's success.

We suggest the team start with the major behaviors and then gradually add other behaviors. For example, if teachers report that Johnny exhibits high rates of kicking, hitting, refusing to follow directions, and screaming, then the target selection should be the behavior(s) that occurs with the greatest frequency and intensity. This process can be analyzed and documented using the Target Behavior Assessment Form shown in Figure 2.

The functional assessment facilitator should also include in the interview documentation pertaining to the physical environments, instructional expectations, and behavioral expectations during which the problem behavior occurs. For instance, if kicking is chosen as the target behavior, the physical environment would include any location where kicking occurs. The instructional expectations would include the instructional demands or academic requirements being placed on the student when the kicking occurs. Behavioral expectations include the behavioral demands pertaining to the environment during the time the kicking behavior occurs.

TARGET BEHAVIOR ASSESSMENT FORM

Teacher   *Mrs. Guess*   Student   *Mark Marks*   Date   *5/1/99*

List problem behaviors exhibited by student:
1. *Inappropriate comments made to other students and teachers*
2. *Cursing, swearing, and threatening teachers and students*

Write a detailed description of one problem behavior:
Tom arrived to class tardy. He began threatening the teacher saying, "you better not write me up again." When confronted by the teacher as to why he was late, he began yelling, and cursing at the teacher and left the room.

Describe the physical environment where the behavior occurs:
Behaviors occur mostly in social studies and English classes. Both classes are in the afternoon after lunch.

List the instructional expectations of the class in which the behavior occurs:
Students are expected to actively participate in their learning by listening in class to the teacher, taking notes, completing daily class assignments and homework assignments when assigned. Students are expected to work together in cooperative groups on certain activities and projects.

List the behavioral expectations of the class in which the behavior occurs:
Listen and follow instructions, treat others respectfully, do the work, and no sleeping in class.

Attach and bring to the team meeting:
- Records of behavior occurrences (frequency/duration counts).
- Academic work information and work samples showing the student's academic ability in reading (rate and comprehension), math computation, and written language.

FIGURE 2. Target Behavior Assessment Form.

Step 2. Describe the Problem Behavior

Once you have pinpointed a specific behavior to target, a detailed description of the behavior is required. A clear and specific definition of the target behavior is critical to the success of the functional assessment process. All components throughout the functional assessment process will refer back to the definition of the target behavior either directly or indirectly. Merely saying that the student "talks out" or is "off task" is not a complete description of the behavior. What does the behavior look like? A clear description of the behavior means identifying the behavior in words that everybody, including the student, can understand.

Behavior must be defined in clear and observable terms. For example, if the target behavior is "talking out," this might be described as "talking in class while the teacher is presenting the lesson without raising your hand and being called on by the teacher," or "blurting out answers without raising hand." Off-task behavior may be described as "talking to other students when the teacher is presenting the lesson" or "not working on assignment when assigned." All persons involved need to have an understanding of what the behavior is and the conditions describing the behavior. You need to know specifically what it is you are observing for data collection purposes.

Other examples of student behaviors that might be identified as problem behaviors include passive (internalizing) behaviors such as refusal to do work, ignoring teacher directions, being inattentive, irritable, and daydreaming, or aggressive and destructive (externalizing) behaviors such as throwing a pencil across the classroom, swearing, cursing, arguing or hitting another student (Coleman, 1992; Hallahan & Kauffman, 1994). Many behaviors exhibited by students with mild disabilities can be listed under five major categories: (a) aggression, (b) inappropriate talk, (c) noncompliance, (d) off-task, and (e) self-injurious behavior. These categories are outlined in Table 1. Internalizing behaviors generally come under the categories of noncompliance and off-task, whereas externalizing behaviors come under aggression and inappropriate talk. To ensure that selected target behaviors are appropriate, teachers should ask themselves the following questions:

1. How important is the behavior to the success of this student and others in my classroom?
2. Does the behavior occur exclusively in the classroom or does it occur in other settings?
3. Does the behavior affect the student's learning?
4. Does the behavior harm the student and/or others?

Once you have identified and defined the behavior, you are ready to determine the frequency, intensity, and duration of the behavior, the antecedents and the consequences of the behavior, and other relevant information about the student's behavior in the context (environment) where it occurs.

ASSESSMENT MEASURES

Functional assessment uses multiple assessment measures to assess student behavior and to make decisions about the problem behavior. This section

TABLE 1. Target Behaviors

Aggression	Inappropriate Talk	Noncompliance	Off-Task	Self-Injurious
■ hitting, biting, spitting, pushing, scratching, kicking, shoving	■ talking out	■ failure to comply with teacher request or instruction	■ out-of-seat without permission/ wandering about the room	■ head banging
■ throwing objects	■ talking back to teacher	■ refusal to follow adult authority	■ not following directions	■ biting or chewing on self
■ destruction of property	■ negative comments	■ refusal to follow classroom/building policies	■ conducting non-school business	■ using objects (pen, pencils, scissors, etc.) to cut or puncture self
■ leaving school/room	■ swearing	■ failure to begin task when asked	■ touching others	■ consuming nonedible substances
■ hitting objects against desk, wall, floor	■ bullying	■ doing nothing	■ talking to other students	■ vomiting
■ temper tantrums	■ yelling	■ refusal to talk	■ no materials	■ skin-tearing
■ fighting	■ making inappropriate sounds	■ ignoring teacher directions	■ not working when assigned	■ hair pulling
■ advancements made to others	■ questioning teacher's authority	■ working on non-school materials	■ attention-seeking behaviors	■ biting or sucking body parts
■ destroying school objects such as paper, pencil, books, assignments	■ inappropriate comments	■ putting head down in class	■ looking around the room	■ hitting self
■ bullying	■ verbal refusals	■ verbal refusals	■ gesturing to peers	■ pinching self
■ threats	■ verbal threats	■ sleeping in class	■ daydreaming	■ using objects to injure self
■ hair pulling	■ talking to other students without permission	■ physical refusal	■ playing and fidgeting with objects	■ kicking self
■ attacking others	■ name calling		■ humming or singing	■ skin picking
■ profanity	■ sexual innuendoes		■ preoccupation with other stimuli in the classroom	■ drugs/alcohol
■ inappropriate touching	■ inappropriate symbolism			
■ weapons	■ profanity			
	■ harassing statements			
	■ arguing			

begins with a discussion of the importance of collecting baseline data and then describes in detail several types of data collection measures that can be used to collect data on the student and his or her target behavior. Gathering data as outlined in this section provides important information that can be used when making decisions about the student's behavior.

Step 3. Collect Behavioral Baseline Data and Academic Information

Baseline data. Baseline data is the level of the natural occurrence of the target behavior before intervention (Kerr & Nelson, 1998). During baseline you record the occurrence or nonoccurrence of the target behavior using an identified measurement system such as frequency count, duration recording, or time sampling.

We suggest that you collect a minimum of five consecutive baseline data points by observing and collecting data for five school days. Baseline data are very important to the functional assessment process as they give an initial indication of how frequent and intense the behavior is.

Baseline data are used as a comparison with intervention data (interventions and modifications tried) to determine the effectiveness of the intervention or to show if there is a change in the behavior as result of interventions. Kerr and Nelson (1983) described baseline data as a way to provide a standard against which to evaluate program changes. Without assessment prior to the intervention, there is no accurate way to measure the effectiveness of a given intervention.

You can think of baseline data the way you would think of a pretest. That is, data are collected on the target behavior before the intervention is implemented and later compared carefully with the intervention data. This is very important as interventions are being implemented to determine if changes in the behavior occur.

There are different ways to collect baseline and intervention data. The procedures discussed in this section fall in line with the 1997 IDEA Amendments which place emphasis on assessment of student behavior. The following section discusses different ways to measure and collect data when conducting functional assessments.

Data Collection Measures

Data collection of the target behavior is an important piece in the functional assessment process since it helps provide the team with an accurate picture of the student's behavior. Data collection methods that can be used to collect functional assessment information about the student are: direct observation and informal observation.

Direct observation. Direct observation is one component of the functional assessment process. With this method of observation, you record factual information about the student's target behavior in the context where it occurs (classroom or other school-based setting). Direct observations are not assumptions or opinions, they are a collection of concrete objective facts that describe the frequency, intensity, and duration of the behavior. The teacher or other selected person observes the student's behavior and records the occurrence or nonoccurrence of the behavior and writes down information observed about the student's behavior.

There are different ways to observe, record, and collect data. These include: continuous or anecdotal, scatter plot, frequency count, duration recording, interval recording, and momentary time sampling. These measurement procedures can be used when recording both baseline and intervention data. Each of these methods is described below. Kerr and Nelson (1983) identified areas that should be considered when selecting a measurement system.

1. The target behavior
2. The intervention goal. Are you trying to increase or decrease the behavior?
3. Observation setting. Is the behavior being observed in the class, playground, lunch, or during seatwork?
4. The person conducting the observation. Is it the classroom teacher, paraeducator, or other? Have the professionals received training in observation techniques?
5. Time available for observation.

Using the guidelines listed above, select the most appropriate measurement procedure that will yield a clear picture of the frequency, duration, and intensity of the behavior. McConnell, Hilvitz, and Cox (1998) suggested no less than 30 minutes per observation period when collecting baseline and intervention data.

Formal Recording Measures

There are a variety of recording measures to select from when making student observations. This section discusses and provides examples of five different recording measures that can be used to collect data on the student's target behavior. Instruction in how to collect data using each of the measures is presented.

Continuous or anecdotal recording. Anecdotal recording involves recording the behavior in a written narrative as it occurs. In other words, you write down word for word what you see. Figure 3 shows an example of an anecdotal recording form. This method allows the observer to capture what occurred prior to the behavior (the antecedent), the behavior, and the outcome or consequence that resulted as a result of the behavior. Some very useful information can be captured about the student's behavior in the environment where it occurs using this method.

Anecdotal methods of data collection provide information that can be used when determining the target behavior. But although some important and useful information about the behavior(s) in question can be gathered with anecdotal recording, this is not a method you would use alone to collect baseline data or intervention data.

Scatter plot. One way to gather information about when the behavior occurs is to complete a scatter plot. This recording approach can be used to help determine when and where the behavior most likely occurs. The observer, using a specified symbol, indicates whether the behavior occurred in a specified time period. A blank grid indicates that the behavior did not occur.

Using scatter plot observation can reveal insights into certain behavior patterns over time and settings. It can show relationships between problem behaviors

ANECDOTAL RECORDING FORM

Student: _Rosie Donnelly_   Class: _Science_   Activity: _Lab Activity_

School: _Big Hill Jr. High_   Teacher: _Steve Austin_   Date: _4-25-99_

Grade: _7_

Time	Behavior Observed
10:13 A.M.	The target student engaged in excessive movement around the room during free time. She visited loudly with peers and made jokes constantly. Her volume was very high and her laughter was loud and annoying to some students. She was notably more active than classmates.

Time	Behavior Observed
10:30 A. M.	Mr. Austin asked students to come to attention about 10:20 A.M.; however, Rosie continued to flit about the room. She was distracted by PE students who peeked in the room, and one of the basketballs came rolling in. She picked it up and initiated a keep-away game from a boy who ran in the classroom from gym to get it.

Time	Behavior Observed
10:40 A. M.	Mr. Austin reminded Rosie about the lab rules for the sixth time. She finally stood near her table but watched the door where students from PE had been peeking in and talked to students at the table behind her. Then she began balancing her body between the two tables while swinging her legs back and forth.

FIGURE 3. Anecdotal Recording Form.

at certain times of the day. Figure 4 shows a sample scatter plot. Each day is represented by a vertical line that is divided into thirty-minute blocks of time.

Frequency count or event recording. Frequency count or event recording means recording how often a behavior occurs. You simply mark the occurrence of the behavior and tally the number of times it occurs over a specified time. This is the easiest way to collect data and the one used most widely. With this method of recording you can note the number of times the student is out of seat, number of talk-outs or number of inappropriate comments made. Figure 5 is an example of a frequency count or event recording sheet that can be used for frequency recording.

Duration recording. Duration recording measures how long a behavior lasts. You record from the time the behavior starts until it ends. With this method you can record how long the student is out of seat, how long it takes the student to respond to teacher requests, or how long a temper tantrum lasts. The duration can be monitored using a stopwatch, clock, second-hand watch, or counter. Figure 6 shows an example of a duration recording form. This form can also be used to collect the

SCATTER PLOT

Student/Grade _____   School _____   Observer _____

Problem Behavior(s) _____

X = 1–5   O = 6–10

Time	M	T	W	Th	F	M	T	W	Th	F	M	T	W	Th	F	M	T	W	Th	F
Activity																				
7:30–8:00																				
8:00–8:30																				
8:30–9:00																				
9:00–9:30																				
9:30–10:00																				
10:00–10:30																				
10:30–11:00																				
11:00–11:30																				
11:30–12:00																				
12:00–12:30																				
12:30–1:00																				
1:00–1:30																				
1:30–2:00																				
2:00–2:30																				
2:30–3:00																				
3:00–3:30																				
3:30–4:00																				

FIGURE 4. Scatter Plot.

FREQUENCY COUNT RECORDING

Student___*Tom Clark*___   Behavior___*Destroys assignments*___

Observer___*Sue Best*___   Class___*Science*___

Mark each time the behavior occurs.   Baseline___*X*___   Intervention_____

Date	Time Observed	Frequency Count
9/17/99	12:20 – 1:00 p.m.	I I I
9/22/99	1:05 – 1:15 p.m.	I I I
9/23/99	1:10 – 1:20 p.m.	I I
9/24/99	1:20 – 1:30 p.m.	I I I
9/25/99	1:15 – 1:25 p.m.	I I I

Comments: Behaviors occur more frequently during the second half of the class period when asked to complete assignments.

FIGURE 5. Frequency Count Recording

DURATION AND A-B-C OBSERVATION FORM

Baseline ___X___

Student _Tom Clark_   Behavior _Destroys assignments_   Observer _Sue Best_   Intervention ___

Date	Time	Length of Behavior	What Occurred Prior to the Behavior	Describe Behavior	Outcome of Behavior
9/17/99	1:20–1:30 p.m.	20–30 seconds	The students were assigned independent seatwork. The teacher gave individual help to students as she walked around the classroom. The teacher was standing at Tom's desk.	Tom wads up his paper, then tears it up and throws the pieces to the floor.	Other students turn to look. The teacher says to Tom, "Get out another sheet of paper and start over." She waits at his desk another 45 seconds.
9/22/99	1:15 p.m.	15 seconds	Verbal instructions were given on how to complete a pre-lab worksheet.	Tom wads up his paper and clenches it in his fist.	Several students turn to look at Tom. The teacher tells him the work must be completed by the end of class or he will have to stay after school.
9/23/99	1:00–1:10 p.m.	25 seconds	The class completed watching a film.	Tom picks up his paper in one hand, then puts his head on his desk and wads up his paper.	The teacher tells Tom to sit up, straighten out his worksheet, and get to work.
9/24/99	1:15–1:25 p.m.	20 seconds	Students were assigned to answer questions from their book after viewing a teacher demonstration.	Tom takes out a sheet of paper. He starts to write, then wads up his paper and slams his book shut.	A few students giggle. Some turn to look. The teacher says, "Tom, you are wasting time."
9/25/99	1:05–1:15 p.m.	25 seconds	Students completed oral review questions and were given directions to complete a review study guide for a test.	Tom receives his study guide, looks at it, and separates the pages. He then wads up each page, one at a time, loudly.	The teacher tells Tom to take his things and go to the office.

FIGURE 6. Duration and A-B-C Observation Form

antecedent-behavior-consequence (A-B-C) observations. Making A-B-C observations involves observing and recording events that occur immediately prior to the student's target behavior, a description of the behavior, and what happens immediately after the occurrence of the behavior itself (Kerr & Nelson, 1998).

Interval recording. For interval recording observation, periods are broken down into small time intervals such as 10, 15, or 20 seconds, and you observe and note whether the behavior occurred or did not occur during the specified interval. When using this method of recording, you can measure the occurrence of the behavior continuously during the observation period or you can record whether the behavior occurred during the observation interval. This method requires the full attention of the person observing.

For use of recording, behavior codes for interval recording can be as simple as "(+)" for occurrence and "(o)" for nonoccurrence. If out of seat is the target behavior, the observer may choose to mark "(S)" for the behavior code in the appropriate cell if the student was observed in seat or "(OT)" for out of seat. With this recording method you can observe more than one behavior at a time. Interval recording is an effective measure to use when recording behaviors that tend to occur more frequently such as "talk-outs," "off-task," and "out-of-seat behaviors." Figure 7 shows an interval and time sampling data collection form. Interval recording is reported in percentages and is calculated by dividing the total number of intervals by the number of intervals during which behavior occurred × 100 (Kerr & Nelson, 1983). This calculation gives you the percentage of the occurrence of the behavior.

Time sampling. Time sampling procedures record the occurrence or nonoccurrence of the behavior at the end of a specified time period. For example, during a 30-minute observation period the behavior is recorded at 20-second intervals. That is, the behavior is recorded only if the student is engaged in the behavior at the end of the interval, unlike interval recording, in which you record if the behavior occurred at all. If the observer is limited in the amount of time to observe the student, then time sampling may be an appropriate measure to use. Also, when continuous observation of the behavior is not feasible because of the class activity, setting, time, etc., time sampling may be appropriate (Kerr & Nelson, 1983).

Practitioners may also wish to utilize Greenwood, Carta, Kamps, Terry, and Delquadri (1994) EBASS computerized technology for collecting data using interval time sampling. With the EBASS system, observers collect data on the target behavior with the assistance of a laptop computer. The observer is prompted with a soft "beep" sound for the events to be recorded using a look, record, and rest sequence. At that time, the observer records the behavior based on only a brief observation. The data are compiled in a comprehensive graph and written summarization that can assist the functional assessment process.

We suggest that you select the most effective measurement system applicable to the student's behavior and setting that yields the most useful information about the student's behavior. Some of the measurement methods described here can be combined, such as frequency, duration, and time sampling; they are easy and effective ways to measure both frequent and infrequent behaviors.

INTERVAL AND TIME SAMPLING OBSERVATION SHEET

Teacher_____Student _____Grade_____

Observer_____Time started _____Time ended _____

Behavior _____Activity_____Date _____

Recording Codes: + = Occurrence   Baseline_____   Intervention _____
                     o = Nonoccurrence

                                              Observation Intervals: 10   20   30
                                                                                  (seconds)

FIGURE 7. Interval and Time Sampling Observation Sheet

Reporting Data

Graphing and charting and looking at the results of the data visually is part of the data collection process. By looking at the data, one can easily detect the frequency and intensity of the behavior and note any changes in the behavior. Different types of graphs can be used to record behavior. Regardless of the type of graph or chart selected, they all serve three important purposes (Kerr & Nelson 1998):

1. They summarize data in a manner convenient for precise, daily decision making.
2. They communicate program effects.
3. They provide reinforcement and feedback to those persons involved with the program.

Sample data graphing forms that can be used to record baseline and intervention data are presented in Figures 8, 9, and 10. Figure 8 shows the percentage of occurrence of the behavior, and Figure 9 shows the number of occurrences. Figure 10 can be used to record the number of times the behavior occurs and the numbers can be connected to form a line graph.

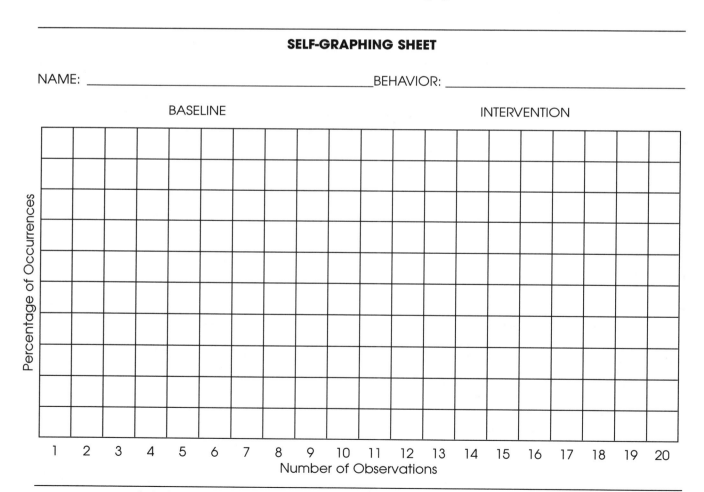

FIGURE 8. Self-Graphing Sheet (Percentage of Occurrences)

SELF-GRAPHING SHEET

NAME: _____ BEHAVIOR: _____

Beginning Date: _____ Ending Date: _____

BASELINE   INTERVENTION(S)

Number of Occurrences

1 2 3 4 5 6 7 8 9 10 11 12 13 14 15 16 17 18 19 20

OBSERVATION DAYS

FIGURE 9. Self-Graphing Sheet (Number of Occurrences)

BEHAVIOR OBSERVATION GRAPHING SHEET

Name: _____   Behavior: _____

Circle the number of times the behavior occurs for each date.
Connect circles to form graph.

BASELINE _____   INTERVENTION(S) – – – – – –

Observation Days

Intervention(s): _____

FIGURE 10. Behavior Observation Graphing Sheet

Data collected using direct observation methods are reviewed and analyzed by the educational team and used to develop a hypothesis (Step 7). This information is also used when developing the Behavioral Intervention Plan.

Informal Methods

In addition to direct observation, informal methods of data collection provide vital information about the student that is useful to the functional assessment process. This method of data collection allows the team to gather specific information about the student from multiple sources (teachers, family members, and peers).

Informal methods include interviews, checklists, behavior rating scales, questionnaires, IEP review, academic information and assessment, school discipline reports, medical reports, report cards, and reports from current and past teachers.

You may choose from a number of commercial forms (checklists, behavior rating scales, and questionnaires) in addition to the forms presented in this publication to gather specific information about the problem behavior. This section discusses the importance of gathering information from student interviews, parent interviews, academic assessments, and medical information to include in the functional assessment.

Student Interview. The purpose of conducting student interviews is to gain information about the student's perspective of the occurrence of the problem behavior. Through this method of assessment, many times the student can tell you why the behavior is occurring.

The team selects the most appropriate person to interview the student. For example, if the student is in conflict with a specific person on the team, that person should not be selected to conduct the interview. The interviewer interviews the student face to face about the problem behavior(s) using a structured, preplanned format. (See Figure 11). If appropriate, this can be done in a private conference with the student and the interviewer.

In some cases, depending on the severity of the behavior in question, it may be appropriate for more than one person to be involved in the interview process. For example, for those students who have known or suspected tendencies of physically aggressive behavior or if the target behavior is aggression, it is best practice to have another adult present to provide assistance if needed (e.g., restraint, getting help from others, calling designated persons) if the student becomes harmful to herself or himself or to the interviewer.

In addition, it may be helpful to have another person there to observe, take notes, and listen for specific "triggers" that may be contributing to the student's behavior. Thus, observations from a second person can provide information about the student's perspective that the observer may not otherwise note. This additional information may be helpful and lead to a more precise assessment of the function of the student's behavior.

The interviewer should ask questions that address when the behavior occurs and why it occurs. It is important to encourage the student to answer the questions honestly and thoroughly. At some point during the interview, discuss how the behavior is affecting the student's academic progress in school.

STUDENT INTERVIEW FORM

Name: *Tom Clark*   Date: *9/11/99*

Interviewer:_____   Class: _____

Complete with student.

1. What things do you generally do that get you in trouble at school?

    Sometimes I don't do my work. I get mad and tear things up. I might throw my book on the floor if I get really mad.

2. What are you doing when the behavior occurs and what usually happens afterward?

    I'm supposed to be reading or writing something. The teacher gets mad at me and I might have to stay after school or go to the principal.

3. When and where do the behaviors generally occur?

    Mostly in science class.

4. How would you describe your behavior at school?

    Well, if I can work in a group or have a helper, I think I do O.K. I get along with most everybody. But it's hard to understand what to do if I have to read everything.

5. What do you do when you get angry?

    I just feel all tight and mad. I just want to get rid of all my work. I don't feel like doing what I'm told.

6. What do you like most about school?

    I like doing work with my friends. I like watching films or looking at pictures. I like having a partner. I like art class.

7. What things do you not like to do at school?

    Read. Write. Having to do things by myself.

8. What teacher behavior especially bothers you?

    I don't like my teacher to tell me what to do or to say something that makes me feel stupid.

9. What are your favorite classes?

    Art and Shop classes.

10. What classes are hard for you?

    Science — sometimes and Reading

11. What can your teachers do to help you be more successful at school?

    Well, my Art teacher and Shop teacher show me pictures or something so I can see what my work is supposed to look like. There isn't very much reading or writing.

12. List some things you do best:

    Collect things. Draw things. Make things.

Additional Comments:

Tom appeared a little nervous at first about answering questions from an adult. After verbally reassuring him that we were trying to find a better way to help him learn, he answered questions as asked. He said he was worried someone might get mad at him.

FIGURE 11. Student Interview Form.

Guidelines to follow when conducting a student interview:

1. Arrange for an individual time and place to meet with the student.
2. Allow a minimum of 20 minutes for the interview.
3. Discuss the behavior and how it is affecting the student's progress in school.
4. Avoid questions that allow the student to respond with "I don't know."
5. Gather as much information as you can about the student's perception of the behavior in question.

Parent Interviews. Interviewing parents about their child can also provide valuable information to the functional assessment. The following are a list of the types of questions that should be asked during the parent interview.

1. What is a "normal" day for the child at home?
2. How does your child respond to changes?
3. Have there been significant changes in the home (such as someone leaving, death, additions, siblings, grandparents, an illness, or job changes)?
4. Has your child expressed any fears?
5. What does your child enjoy doing?
6. What is rewarding to your child?
7. How do you discipline your child?
8. How would you describe your child's friends?
9. Is there something that your child continually comments about regarding home, school, or an event?
10. What is important to you as a parent as it relates to your child?
11. What concerns do you have about your child?
12. Have you noticed anything unusual about your child lately?

The parent interview can take place in a formal or informal setting as determined by the team. Parent interviews can also provide valuable information to the team about the student as they write the Behavior Intervention Plan.

Academic Information and Assessment. Is the problem behavior related to academic instruction? Is the curriculum appropriate? Is the teacher teaching at the appropriate instructional level? Does the student have the prerequisite skills needed to complete assignments? These are important questions that need to be answered during the functional assessment process. If the class work is below or above the student's ability level, this may be the triggering factor that leads to behavior issues.

Gathering academic information about the student's performance provides the functional assessment team with information that can assist in determining if the curriculum is related to the behavior or if the behavior is the result of the student's skill or performance deficits. Some problem behaviors may be the result of frustration that is brought on by the fact that the student does not have the prerequisite skills needed to do the work. The class work may be too difficult for the student. That is why it is important to know if the behavior is related to academics.

If the team discovers that the curriculum is a contributing factor to the student's behavior, this information can be useful when selecting interventions to be tried with student. For instance, some students may require interventions such as academic, curriculum, and instructional modifications and accommodations, peer assistance, and a variety of instructional options.

Academic information collected by the classroom teacher should include:

1. The student's ability levels in reading (regular rate and reading comprehension)
2. Math (computational skills)
3. Written language (writing samples)
4. Work samples related to the setting

Medical information. When conducting a functional assessment, a review of the student's medical information should always be considered. Team members probe to determine if medical factors are in some way related to the occurrence of the student's problem behavior. Medical issues that need to be addressed include:

1. Is the student on medication(s)?
2. Are there side effects to the medicine?
3. Is the medicine being monitored and distributed appropriately?
4. What is the date of the last medical exam?
5. Does the student see a doctor regularly? If so, for what?
6. Is there a medical diagnosis?
7. How is the student's vision and hearing?
8. Are there other health concerns?

These are important questions that need to be addressed at the team meeting. Completing a medical assessment form such as shown in Figure 12 can provide important information to teams as they make decisions about possible causes that may be affecting the student's behavior.

Step 4. Describe the Environment and Setting Demands

Collecting data about the classroom environment and student expectations is another informal assessment source that can provide valuable information. As noted earlier, the functional assessment facilitator collects this information or designates someone else on the team to do so. This step involves collecting information on environmental and setting demands that affect the student. This includes the identification and description of environmental factors, as well as the teacher's instructional and behavioral expectations for the student in the setting in which the identified behavior usually occurs.

The Educational and Environmental Analysis presented in Figure 13 is a form that can be used to collect information about the student in the classroom environment. Information gathered by means of this form can provide the team with valuable information that can be used when they develop a Behavior Intervention Plan for the student. The description of the environment and setting demands should include information such as:

1. A description of the physical environment (where does the student sit in proximity to the teacher, the chalkboard, etc.?).

MEDICAL ASSESSMENT FORM

Name _Samuel Swimming_   Date _1-25-99_   Grade _2nd_

School _Brightwater Elementary_   D.O.B. _6-5-90_   Age _8_

Person(s) completing form   _Noah Arks, Ed.S. (school psychologist)_

    Date of Last Physical Examination: _6-3-98_

    Vision Results: _Passed: 20/20 R & L with glasses_

    Hearing Results: _Passed_

1. Medical diagnosis (if any):
   Attention Deficit Hyperactivity Disorder (ADHD)

2. Does the medical diagnosis have an effect on the student's behavior?
   Yes. The student demonstrates significant off-task behaviors and excessive movement.

3. Is the student on medication?
   Yes

4. What type?
   Ritalin

5. Are there side effects to the medication? Describe.
   Yes. The parent reports the student is up all night, and the teacher reports the student is not eating lunch.

6. Are there questions about the side effects?
   Yes. 1. The team wants to know if the student's inability to sleep at night is the result of a medication side effect or if the problem is the result of an inappropriate sleep/wake schedule.
   2. What does the doctor say about the student's lack of appetite at lunchtime?

7. How and with whom is the medication administered?
   The parent administers the medication before breakfast in the morning; by the school nurse before lunch in the afternoon; and again by the parent before dinner in the evening.

FIGURE 12. Medical Assessment Form.

EDUCATIONAL AND ENVIRONMENTAL ANALYSIS

Teacher: *Steve Austin*   Course Subject: *Science*   Grade: *7*   Type of Classroom: *Laboratory*

School: *Big Hill Jr. High*   Classroom Location: *Basement*   Length of Class: *50 minutes*   No. of Students in Class: *24*

Interviewer: *Babs Walters, Ed.S. (School Psychologist)*   Date: *4-19-99*

1. CLASSROOM ENVIRONMENT

Describe your classroom set-up and student seating arrangement:

Students are seated at lab tables, two to a table. All tables face the lecture/backboard area. Tables are arranged in horizontal rows: three across.

Identify distractors:

1. Wooden floors and high ceilings make for loud echoes.
2. The gymnasium is directly across from the lab and the boiler room is next door. These factors increase noise levels.
3. The PE teacher doesn't have control and students come to lab from PE with balls and equipment, trying to see their friends.

2. CLASSROOM MANAGEMENT

What are the classroom rules?

1. sit quietly
2. face the front
3. raise hand to speak
4. do not begin experiment until directed

What are the consequences for breaking classroom rules?

I tell them to, "stop and think about the rules in lab".

How do you handle student conflicts and/or discipline issues?

I handle them myself, right there in lab. If my students misbehave, they are not allowed to do the assignment and get an F for the Day. I do not allow make up or extra credit. It's their problem.

3. INSTRUCTIONAL DELIVERY

What instructional methods do you use?

1. lecture
2. workbook
3. demonstration
4. visual aids (overhead, drawing, models)
5. guided practice

What does a class period generally consist of?

All of the above, except on days we have written tests. Then, that's all we do.

Are students given free time during your class period? If so, how much and what activities do they engage in?

Yes. When they first come in, I give them about 10 minutes of free time, because I am still cleaning up from the previous class.

How do you work with students in your classroom?

I teach and demonstrate the activity and then circulate the room. I help each student as needed and monitor the whole class that way.

4. COURSE REQUIREMENTS

What are students required to do in your class?

They complete weekly quizzes and unit tests for about 50 % of their grade. The rest of the grade is based on class participation, workbook assignments, and experiments.

What materials and supplies are needed by students?

I supply everything, even the pencils. Workbooks are kept here in class.

(continues next page)

FIGURE 13.   Educational and Environmental Analysis.

How much class participation is required by students?
A lot of participation is required in my class.

What skills do students need to be successful in your class-room?

They need to have only a basic - very basic, as in almost nothing back-ground in science. Really I start from scratch with them and give them everything - all the information they need to be successful. All they need is good listening skills and the willingness to learn.

5. CLASS ASSIGNMENTS
What types of assignments are given?
General science/lab workbook lessons and general lab experiments.

Describe frequency of assignments:
Students are assigned workbook assignments almost daily.

How are directions presented?
1. verbally
2. with overhead or on blackboard
3. demonstration

What are your homework requirements?
None

6. INSTRUCTIONAL MATERIALS
Title of textbook used:
Workbook: Our Living World

What supplemental instructional materials are used?
Science lab materials

What modifications are made for students with disabilities?
I didn't make any modifications. Our school has a special aide who fol-lows students with disabilities to my class. She takes my materials ahead of time and prepares students in advance. She works individu-ally with them in my class as needed.

7. GRADING SYSTEM
What kinds of tests are given?
Fill in the blank and multiple-choice

How often?
Quizzes are given every Friday and unit tests are given about once a month.

What is your make-up policy for assignments, homework, and tests?

There is no make up for assignments so attendance is crucial. Make up tests are allowed with a written request from the student.

Describe your grading criteria:

90-100% = A
80-89% = B
70-79% = C
60-69% = D
50-below = F

8. TEACHER BEHAVIORS
What do you like about your class?
1. I like being around the students – it keeps me feeling young.
2. I like the fact that I've been doing this for years. I can teach the lessons with my eyes closed. I don't have to prepare.

What do you like about the curriculum you teach?

My own adaptation of the book. If there are parts I don't like, I can leave them out and focus on the important parts.

Is there anything you would change about the way you con-duct your class?

Yes, I'd be able to conduct it in a new lab away from the gym.
I'd steer away from my testing style, but I don't know any other way.

FIGURE 13. (Continued).

2. A description of the classroom management procedures (what are the classroom rules) and behavioral expectations. Is the student expected to raise hand before speaking or is the student expected to work cooperatively in groups, independently, or with partners?).

3. A description of instructional expectations (is the student expected to take notes from lecture or is the student expected to read and comprehend information contained in the sixth-grade social studies text?).

4. A description of instructional delivery methods (does the teacher lecture, co-teach, use different instructional methods?).

5. A description of the types of assignments/homework and tests given (how are directions presented?).

Step 5. Complete the Functional Assessment Interview Form

This step is to be completed at a planned functional assessment team meeting. This meeting is designed to review data and gather additional information about the target behavior in an attempt to gain a better understanding about the function of the student's behavior.

The educational team (e.g., IEP, behavior intervention, student improvement, and preassessment) led by the functional assessment facilitator or designated person knowledgeable about the functional assessment process interviews the classroom teacher(s) during the team meeting. Specific questions related to the student's behavior and its relationship to the classroom environment will be probed.

The functional assessment interview form developed by the authors is divided into four sections that:

A. describe the behavior
B. define setting events and environmental factors that predict the behavior
C. define specific immediate antecedent events that predict when the behaviors are most likely to occur
D. identify specific consequences that follow the behavior

Purpose of the Functional Assessment Interview Form

The purpose of the Functional Assessment Interview form (Figure 14) is to gather information about the student's behavior by providing a structured way to gather and review information about the student in more detail. Through this process, a broad base of information about the student's behavior is obtained. Behavior is assessed in the classroom or school environment where it occurs. Information gathered from this form is used to help make assumptions about the student's behavior.

The authors strongly suggest completing this form as part of the team meeting. We find that it is very helpful for other team members to hear the information shared about the student as it ensures that the form is completed with the necessary information. Completion of the Functional Assessment Interview form takes about 20 minutes and should be incorporated as part of the meeting time. To be timely in conducting the interview, it is important that the person leading the

FUNCTIONAL ASSESSMENT INTERVIEW FORM

Student _____ Teacher _____

Team Member's Name   Team Member's Position

_____ _____

_____ _____

_____ _____

_____ _____

A. Describe the Behavior:

    1. What is the behavior?

    2. How is the behavior performed?

    3. How often does the behavior occur?

    4. How long does the behavior last when it occurs?

    5. What is the intensity of the behavior when it occurs?

B. Define Setting Events and Environmental Factors That Predict the Behavior (describe the following variables):

    1. Classroom structure (physical).

    2. Class rules and procedural expectations.

    3. Instructional delivery (lecture, cooperative learning, labs, etc.).

    4. Instructional materials (textbooks, worksheets, hands-on activities).

    5. How are directions presented?

    6. Assessment techniques (multiple-choice tests, essay tests, rubrics, authentic assessment).

FIGURE 14. Functional Assessment Interview Form.   *(continues next page)*

C. Define Specific Immediate Antecedent Events That Predict When the Behaviors Are Most Likely to Occur:

1. When are the behaviors most likely to occur?

2. When are the behaviors least likely to occur?

3. Where are the behaviors most likely to occur?

4. Where are the behaviors least likely to occur?

5. During what activities are the behaviors most likely to occur?

6. During what activities are the behaviors least likely to occur?

D. Identify Specific Consequences That Follow the Behavior:

1. What specific consequence is most likely to immediately follow the behavior?

2. What seems to be the effect of the consequence on the student's behavior?

3. Does the consequence remove the student from an uncomfortable situation?

4. Is there consistency between the consequences given by the classroom teacher and the consequences given by the administrators?

5. Is there consistent follow-through with all consequences both in the classroom and in the school office?

FIGURE 14. (Continued).

interview is very knowledgeable about the interview questions and is skilled at keeping the interview moving.

Using the interview form, the team will ask many questions in an effort to identify environmental, instructional, and behavioral antecedents and consequences. The functional assessment interview form is a useful tool to get at the core questions associated with the student's behavior. For many teams this is a crucial awakening as they begin to get a clear picture of what is causing the behavior. Figure 15 shows an example of a completed interview. The functional assessment interview process should help to answer questions such as:

1. Does the behavior occur when the student is asked to do something?
2. Does the behavior occur when the student is asked to stop doing something?
3. Does the behavior occur during certain activities?
4. Does the behavior occur during certain types of instruction?
5. Does the behavior occur in the morning or afternoon?

Also during the team meeting, team members led by the team facilitator should review the student's assessed academic skill level, work samples and tests, and medical information, and identify predictors of the behavior (environmental factors, antecedents, and consequences) that can be manipulated in order to affect the student's behavior.

Step 6. Develop a Hypothesis

The next step in the functional assessment process is to develop a hypothesis statement. The hypothesis statement is a summary statement that describes how the behavior is related to the environment. In other words, it describes the relationship between the behavior and the environment (Foster-Johnson & Dunlap, 1993).

Using the information collected during steps 1-5, the team will carefully analyze factors surrounding the student's behavior by paying close attention to the antecedents (what occurred prior to the behavior) and consequences (outcome of the behavior) of the behavior. This information will be used to help the team develop a hypothesis that describes those factors that assist in determining the occurrence (the frequency, duration, and/or intensity) of the problem behavior. Knowing the condition under which the behavior occurs is important.

The team pays close attention to those variables most likely to affect or trigger the student's problem behavior. The team must reach a consensus regarding the function(s) related to the student's behavior (see Table 2 for examples of hypothesis statements). Merely describing the behavior is not enough. It is important to look beyond the behavior and look closely at the function of the behavior. There must be an understanding of the function of the behavior. For example, what is it in the environment that may be triggering or causing the behavior? The environment is what the team will seek to manipulate in order to create changes in the behavior (Foster-Johnson & Dunlap, 1993). The hypothesis answers "why" the student is engaging in the behavior. You can develop more than one hypothesis. The hypothesis guides the development of the Behavior Intervention Plan.

SAMPLE
FUNCTIONAL ASSESSMENT INTERVIEW FORM

Student:___*Tom Clark*___   Teacher:___*Jennifer Braun*___

Team Member's Name   Team Member's Position

___*Ms. Jones*___   English Teacher

___*Mr. Smith*___   Principal

___*Ms. Clark*___   Mother

___*Ms. Johnson*___   Case Manager

A. Describe the Behavior:

1. What is the behavior?

   Tom destroys his written assignments.

2. How is the behavior performed?

   When given written assignments to be completed independently, Tom wads up and/or tears up his paper. When he is reminded to get to work, he says that he does not want to do the work.

3. How often does the behavior occur?

   The behavior occurs on days when written work is to be completed, 3–4 days a week.

4. How long does the behavior last when it occurs?

   15–30 seconds.

5. Describe the intensity of the behavior when it occurs?

   The behavior results in destruction of paper and detracts from peer work time.

B. Define Setting Events and Environmental Factors That Predict the Behavior (describe the following variables):

1. Classroom structure (physical).

   Science 7 is a classroom with work tables and storage cabinets for lab equipment/materials. Students are seated at tables with partners. Tom is not seated with a partner.

2. Class rules and procedural expectations.

   Instructional delivery consists of students responsible for the care of all materials, including their work. Written work must be completed before lab work can begin.

3. Instructional delivery (lecture, cooperative learning, labs, etc.).

   Lecture, cooperative group work, discussion, lab activities, and independent seat work.

4. Instructional materials (textbooks, worksheets, hands on activities).

   Textbook and/or worksheets.

FIGURE 15. Sample — Functional Assessment Interview Form.   *(continues next page)*

5. How are directions presented?

   The teacher gives verbal directions. Some directions are read independently by the students.

6. Assessment techniques (multiple-choice tests, essay tests, rubrics, authentic assessment).

   A multiple-choice test is given weekly. One essay question is included in each test. Each test covers a combination of lab work and written work.

C. Define Specific Immediate Antecedent Events That Predict When the Behaviors Are Most Likely to Occur:

1. When are the behaviors most likely to occur?

   The behaviors generally occur after the lecture and prior to independent seatwork.

2. When are the behaviors least likely to occur?

   The behaviors occur least when Tom is interacting with his peers and feels a part of the group.

3. Where are the behaviors most likely to occur?

   The behaviors occur frequently in his science class.

4. Where are the behaviors least likely to occur?

   The behaviors are least likely to occur in social settings and in classrooms where Tom is not the only one asked to sit alone.

5. During what activities are the behaviors most likely to occur?

   Behaviors occur most during independent seatwork time when Tom is asked to work alone.

6. During what activities are the behaviors least likely to occur?

   The behaviors occur least during group activities.

D. Identify Specific Consequences That Follow the Behavior:

1. What specific consequence is most likely to immediately follow the behavior?

   Teacher/peer attention. The student receives a "0" for the assignment.

2. What seems to be the effect of the consequence on the student's behavior?

   The effect seems to be somewhat positive in that Tom continues the problem behavior.

3. Does the consequence remove the student from an uncomfortable situation?

   Yes, temporarily. It delays work time and provides attention.

4. Is there consistency between the consequences given by the classroom teacher and the consequences given by the administrators?

   Yes.

5. Is there consistent follow-through with all consequences both in the classroom and in the school office?

   Yes.

FIGURE 15. (Continued).

TABLE 2. Sample Hypothesis Statements

Behavior	Hypothesis
Aggression	When the teacher removes distracting objects from Mary and tells her to sit up and pay attention, she tears her paper, kicks her desk, and throws objects across the room resulting in her removal from class.
Inappropriate Talk	Tom engages in inappropriate talk to the teacher that includes verbal refusals, talking back to teacher, and arguing when he is asked to make corrections on his daily work. He engages in this behavior to escape from a non-preferred activity.
Noncompliance	When John is presented new information without prior knowledge, he refuses to complete his assignments. This results in negative peer and adult attention and avoidance of the task.
Off-Task	Susie stares out the window during math instruction in order to escape from the task. The school psychologist found a severe discrepancy in her numerical operations that may be a contributing factor to her off-task behavior.
Self-Injurious	When George is asked to work on unfamiliar tasks, he engages in self-injurious behavior such as head banging, hitting self, and puncturing self with objects. This behavior results in negative peer attention.

In summary the hypothesis is:

1. Based on the information gathered during steps 1-5.
2. Based on a careful analysis of the data.
3. A summary written statement about the function of the behavior.
4. A summary of assessment results.
5. A prediction about the conditions of the behavior (when the behavior is most likely to occur and consequences that seem to maintain it).
6. Testable (manipulate interventions).

When formulating the hypothesis, include a description of the (a) antecedent, (b) problem behavior, and (c) consequence or outcome of the behavior.

Behavior Intervention Plans

As a result of the new mandate made by IDEA, educators are encouraged to use positive interventions that seek to address problem behaviors and promote positive behavior change. This puts the responsibility on the functional assessment team to focus on identifying and determining positive behavior interventions for each student (Johns, 1998).

Assessing student behavior through the detailed process of functional assessment is crucial to the development of an effective Behavior Intervention Plan (Foster-Johnson & Dunlap, 1993). Behavior Intervention Plans should be proactive and preventive rather than reactive. That is, the best practice is to put interventions in place that address specific behaviors before they occur, thereby preventing the future occurrence of the behavior.

PLANNING FOR BEHAVIOR INTERVENTIONS

This chapter focuses on the development, writing, and implementation of Behavior Intervention Plans as outlined in Steps 7-10:

Step   7. Write the Intervention Plan
Step   8. Implement the Behavioral Intervention Plan
Step   9. Collect Behavioral Data
Step 10. Conduct a Follow-up Team Meeting

Step 7. Write a Behavioral Intervention Plan

The development and writing of the Behavior Intervention Plan should be guided by the information gathered through the functional assessment process (Horner, O'Neil & Flannery, 1993). Thus, after the completion of steps 1-6, the functional assessment team members should have some important and valuable information about the student's behavior and should have an understanding of possible cause(s) of the behavior. As stated by Johns (1998), "How can we best determine an appropriate behavioral intervention plan without assessing the where, why, and when of the particular behavior and providing a thorough description of the behavior, including frequency, intensity, and duration" (p. 103).

After working together collaboratively to generate a hypothesis as to why the behavior is occurring, in step 6, the team now begins the process of writing the Behavior Intervention Plan. Interventions selected must be effective and positive and should always be driven by the hypothesis. Figure 16 shows a Behavior Intervention Plan developed by McConnell et al. (1998).

In writing the Behavior Intervention Plan, it is imperative to address factors that may be causes of the behavior and to replace the inappropriate behavior with a more appropriate behavior. Therefore, behavior interventions should seek to (a) manipulate the antecedents (b) teach alternative behavior(s), (c) implement changes in curriculum and instructional strategies, and (d) modify the physical environment (Gable, Quinn, Rutherford, Howell, 1998; Foster-Johnson & Dunlap, 1993; Quinn et al., 1998).

It cannot be emphasized enough that strategies, interventions, and supports that address the problem behavior must be included in the Behavior Intervention Plan, as it is basically developed, and implemented to reduce the occurrence of inappropriate behavior(s). To be effective, Behavior Intervention Plans should include a written description of specific interventions designed to promote academic and behavioral success. Interventions are individualized and specifically designed to meet the behavioral needs of the student.

The parent and the student (when appropriate) should be included in the development of the Behavior Intervention Plan. General educators should also be active participants in the development of Behavior Intervention Plans for students with disabilities since they will be responsible for implementing many of the interventions. The Behavior Intervention Plan should include:

1. Description of the behavior (target behavior and definition)
2. Baseline data results
3. Hypothesis statement
4. Intervention goal
5. Interventions to be tried
6. Follow-up information and dates
7. Names of persons participating in writing the behavior intervention plan

Select Appropriate Interventions

Before writing a behavior intervention plan, it is helpful for team members to find out what interventions have been tried by the classroom teacher with the student. Were the interventions effective? How were they implemented and for how long? Additionally, the team should also find out what the classroom teacher is presently doing to address the student's behavior problems. This information can be documented on a Behavior Intervention Plan Sheet as shown in Figure 17 and referred to when discussing interventions to be tried.

To assist school personnel in writing appropriate intervention plans, Table 3 identifies clinically proven interventions, techniques, and supports that can be used when writing Behavior Intervention Plans for students whose behaviors fall

BEHAVIOR INTERVENTION PLAN

Student: _____   School: _____

Date Developed: _____   Date Implemented: _____

Grade _____

Baseline Data Results:

Hypothesis Statement:

Type of Intervention Plan: Educational _____   Behavioral _____

Person(s) Responsible for Implementing Plan:

DESCRIPTION OF THE BEHAVIOR:

BEHAVIOR   BEHAVIOR DEFINED

INTERVENTION GOAL:

FIGURE 16. Behavior Intervention Plan.   *(continues next page)*

INTERVENTION PLAN:

1.

2.

3.

4.

5.

WHEN AND WHERE THE PLAN WILL BE IMPLEMENTED:

FIGURE 16. (Continued) *(continues next page)*

INTERVENTION DATA COLLECTION SUMMARY:

Week 1

Week 2

Week 3

FOLLOW-UP AND REVIEW DATE(S):

COMMENTS:

TEAM MEETING PARTICIPANTS:

Name	Position
_____	_____
_____	_____
_____	_____
_____	_____
_____	_____

FIGURE 16. (Continued)

BEHAVIORAL INTERVENTION PLAN SHEET

Please complete this form and bring to the team meeting.

Student	Tom Clark	Teacher	Jennifer Braun	Date	9/10/99
Disability	ADHD	School	Middle School	Grade	7

1. Describe behavioral issues.

   He does not complete assignments, turn in assignments on time, or follow teacher instructions; tears up assignments.

2. What disciplinary actions has the student received for inappropriate behavior?

   Verbal teacher reprimands, office referrals, after-school detentions, suspension.

3. How does the student respond to adults?

   Can respond appropriately, but if his work is challenged or questioned, a verbal confrontation erupts. He becomes loud and states he should not have to do the work.

4. What interventions/strategies have you tried?

   Proximity to Tom, repetition of directions with consequences clearly stated if he does not comply, verbally explaining what he must do to earn a passing grade.

5. How were they implemented?

   Immediate physical proximity, immediate verbal directions. When Tom continued to destroy assignments, he was instructed to go to the principal's office, because the behavior interrupted work and learning time of others.

6. How long were they implemented?

   Since the beginning of the school year, about 3½ weeks.

7. Which interventions were effective?

   Sometimes, giving directions over again — more one to one — helped.

8. Which interventions were not effective?

   Tom is still destroying assignments and failing. I don't think any are effective for lasting results.

9. What are you currently doing?

   I'm trying to give Tom more one to one help.

10. What would you like to try?

    I would like to find a "system" Tom can use to let me know when he needs help that is not so destructive to everyone's learning.

FIGURE 17. Behavior Intervention Plan Sheet.

TABLE 3. Interventions.

Aggression	Inappropriate Talk	Noncompliance	Off-Task	Self-Injurious
■ Compliance training	■ Teach new/ appropriate/ alternative behaviors	■ Provide choices	■ Environmental modifications	■ Differential reinforcement of other behaviors (DRO)
■ Conflict resolution	■ Self-monitoring/ management	■ Contingency contract	■ Token or point system	■ Differential reinforcement of alternative behaviors (DRA)
■ Life-Space Interviewing	■ Problem solving techniques	■ Differential reinforcement of other behavior (DRO)	■ Self-monitoring/ management	■ Provide brief and frequent time-outs for increased opportunity to learn behavior expectations
■ Problem solving techniques	■ Think sheets	■ I-Messages	■ Peer partners/Peer support	■ Habit reversal
■ Think sheets	■ Social skills training	■ Teach to student learning styles	■ Redirection prompts/cues/ signaling	■ Token reinforcement
■ Teach new/ appropriate/ alternative behaviors	■ Contingency contract	■ Compliance training	■ Multiple intelligences	■ Positive reinforcement
■ Provide choices	■ Token economies	■ Teach expectations	■ Curricular modifications/ adaptations/ accommodations	■ Social reinforcement
■ Social skills training to address aggressive behavior	■ Visual and verbal prompts to redirect	■ Redirection	■ Academic restructuring	■ Teach new alternative behaviors
■ Support of school personnel	■ Point sheets	■ Token reinforcement	■ Provide instructional options	■ Redirection
■ Stress ball	■ Conferencing	■ Social reinforcement	■ Teach to student learning styles	■ Stress management
■ Referral to other agencies	■ Differential Reinforcement of Other behavior (DRO)	■ Enrich the environment with increased time-in	■ Remove distracting objects/stimuli	■ Sensory reinforcement
■ Crises intervention	■ Positive reinforcement	■ Frequent/brief time-outs with increased opportunities to learn and practice behavior expectations	■ Proximity control	■ Increase and enrich time-in
■ I-Messages	■ Modeling	■ Self-management techniques	■ Hurdle help	
■ Relaxation techniques	■ Increase attention To appropriate talk	■ Withdrawal	■ Break tasks into small segments	
■ Refocus area to cool down	■ Brief time-outs used with other interventions	■ Extinction		
■ Modeling				
■ De-escalation techniques				
■ Anger control				

under the categories of (a) aggression, (b) inappropriate talk, (c) noncompliance, and (d) self-stimulation. As noted, some interventions overlap.

If a student has problems with anger, the Behavior Intervention Plan should incorporate strategies and techniques that teach students alternative ways to deal with situations that makes them angry and frustrated. For example, Tom, who exhibits anger outbursts in his science class when his science teacher gives directions to the class to complete individual written work, wads up (or tears up) his paper. When his teacher asks him why this happens, he says that he does not want to do the work and should not have to do it. When the teacher approaches Tom and tells him to get to work, they usually have a verbal confrontation.

After careful review of the baseline data, observations, teacher information (academic, behavior, and environmental setting demands), interviews, etc., the team reviews and analyzes the data to determine possible causes for the behavior in the context where it occurs. The team hypothesizes that Tom's behavior is related to frustration brought on by a discrepancy between his skill level and the skill level necessary to complete the science assignments. In addition, the team determines that the probable function of Tom's destructive behavior in this specific setting (his science class) is related to the seating arrangement: Tom is isolated from his peers in the classroom, because his teacher felt he could work better at a table by himself. The team then develops an intervention plan to address these specific concerns. Figure 18 shows a sample of what a Behavior Intervention Plan might look like for Tom.

Time-Out. As noted, time-out is listed as an intervention in Table 3. If used correctly and paired with a positive intervention, time-out can be an effective technique (Johns & Carr, 1995). Time-out is a behavior management technique that has been used in special education to help students with mild to severe disabilities gain control over their behavior, namely, aggressive and acting-out behavior. In cases where time-out is the intervention of choice, it should never be used alone and should be used with much caution as it is considered an aversive technique.

Keep in mind that time-out alone is not sufficient to change behavior. The main purpose of conducting the functional assessment is to select positive behavior intervention strategies, interventions, and supports that aim at improving student behavior and promote positive behavioral outcomes for students with disabilities. Time-out should be paired with a positive intervention that encourages positive behaviors. Further, teachers must also be trained in the correct use of time-out procedures. Whenever a time-out procedure is selected as an intervention technique the following procedures must be in place (Johns & Carr, 1995):

1. The school administrator or teacher must notify the parent(s) that this procedure will be used.
2. Students must be informed about the specific behaviors that will lead to time-out before the procedure is used.
3. Students must be given a warning before time-out is implemented.
4. Following the use of time-out, the student must be given the chance to clarify the behavior that led to time-out and to identify and practice alternative behaviors.
5. Time-out procedures must be documented and monitored closely.

SAMPLE
BEHAVIOR INTERVENTION PLAN

Student: *Tom Clark*   School: *Middle School*

Date Developed: *9/30/99*   Date Implemented: *10/3/99*

Grade: *7*

Baseline Data Results:

Tom destroyed assignments 5 out of 5 observation days.

Hypothesis Statement:

Tom's behavior is related to frustration brought on by a discrepancy between his skill level and the skill level necessary to complete the assignments. Much of Tom's destructive behavior is related to his isolated seating from his peers in the classroom. Tom feels singled out because he sits at a table by himself.

Type of Intervention Plan: Educational *X*   Behavioral _____

Person(s) Responsible for Implementing Plan: *Science teacher*

DESCRIPTION OF THE BEHAVIOR:

BEHAVIOR	BEHAVIOR DEFINED
Tom destroys his written assignments.	*Tom wads up and tears up his assignment papers.*

INTERVENTION GOAL:

To decrease the number of occurrences when Tom destroys his assignments to 0 per week.

FIGURE 18. Sample — Behavior Intervention Plan.   *(continues next page)*

INTERVENTION PLAN:

1. *Seat Tom with a peer who has good on-task behavior. The peer will review directions with Tom and assist him in getting started with assignments.*

2. *Provide Tom a daily monitoring assignment checklist to improve areas of difficulty:*

Assignment Checklist

____ *I understood teacher directions*   ____ *I asked for help when I needed it*
____ *I answered all questions*   ____ *I understood the assignment*
____ *I need more time*   ____ *I turned in my assignment*

3. *Provide Tom with academic modifications, including:*

   1. *Extended time to complete and turn in assignments if needed.*
   2. *Outlines, study guides, and graphic organizers provided with textbook assignments to assist Tom in identifying important information.*
   3. *A word/definition list to be used when completing worksheet assignments.*
   4. *Peer assistance with certain assignments.*
   5. *Additional instructional modifications as needed.*

4. *Provide directions to Tom in a variety of ways (verbal, written, direct instruction, and peer assistance).*

5. *Reinforce Tom's academic productivity and assignment completion.*

WHEN AND WHERE THE PLAN WILL BE IMPLEMENTED:

The plan will be implemented in Tom's science class for three consecutive weeks beginning 10/3/99.

FIGURE 18. (Continued)   *(continues next page)*

INTERVENTION DATA COLLECTION SUMMARY:

Week 1   *Decrease in behavior to 3 occurrences.*

Week 2   *Decrease in behavior to 3 occurrences.*

Week 3   *Decrease in behavior to 1 occurrence.*

FOLLOW-UP AND REVIEW DATE(S):

Follow-up and review meeting 10/24/99

COMMENTS:

The intervention plan is successful with Tom.
The team agreed to write the interventions outlined in this plan in Tom's IEP.
The team will meet in 3 weeks for another review.

TEAM MEETING PARTICIPANTS:

Name	Position
_____	_____
_____	_____
_____	_____
_____	_____
_____	_____

FIGURE 18. (Continued)

Cognitive-based interventions. There is a growing research base on the use of cognitive-based interventions. These interventions teach students how to gain control over their own behavior and has been verified empirically as being effective in helping students change their behavior. Using this type of intervention, the student rather than the teacher is in charge of his/her behavior. Cognitive interventions have been shown to increase generalization and maintenance of behaviors and to redirect control within the student. Cognitive interventions include teaching self-monitoring and self-management skills, teaching skills in problem solving, controlling anger, self-instructional training, and resolving conflicts (Dollard, Christen, Colucci, & Epanchin, 1996).

Dollard et al. (1996) described three areas that these cognitive approaches have in common:

1. Students become in charge of their behaviors and gain greater self-control.
2. Students are taught a step-by-step procedure to identify and deal with challenging situations in their lives.
3. Modeling and learning to attend to and control one's internal talk or private speech are part of these interventions.

Considerations When Writing Behavior Intervention Plans

Schools can consider a number of factors when writing Behavior Intervention Plans. When selecting interventions for students, keep in mind that many students with special learning and behavioral needs may be difficult to teach and do not always perform academically as well as other students (Ruhl & Berlinghoff, 1992). In addition, they often bring behaviors that teachers find particularly challenging such as off-task behavior, disruptions, verbal and physical outbursts, and passive and aggressive behavior (Hallahan & Kauffman, 1994; Zaragoza, Vaughn, & McIntosh, 1991).

The team needs to select behavior management techniques and interventions that work by teaching new behaviors that replace inappropriate ones. Therefore, it is important to use instructional approaches and behavioral interventions that have proven successful with these students (Meese, 1994).

When writing Behavior Intervention Plans it is important to consider factors such as (a) the academic and behavioral expectations of the general education teacher, (b) resources that can be accessed, (c) administrative support, (d) the behavioral needs of some students with disabilities, (e) when, where, and how frequent the behavior is occurring, (f) the function or cause of the behavior, (g) school/teacher expectations, (h) teacher skills, (i) the needs of the other students in the classroom, (j) the disability of the student and (k) the skill level of the student.

Behavior Intervention Plans need to be age-appropriate, workable, and reasonable. To be effective, interventions must match the student's behavior. When writing Behavior Intervention Plans, the team must keep in mind the person(s) who will be responsible for implementing the plan. For example, is the classroom teacher knowledgeable about and skilled in how to implement the Behavior Intervention Plan? Or does the classroom teacher need training in how to implement the strategies and interventions written into the Behavior Intervention Plan? Are additional resources and supports needed? Does the classroom teacher need assistance in implementing the Behavior Intervention Plan? For Behavior Intervention Plans to be effective, they must be followed and implemented as written and agreed upon by the team.

Step 8. Implement the Behavioral Intervention Plan

Step 8, the implementation phase of the functional behavior assessment, is one of the most important steps of the functional assessment process. This is where the classroom teacher or designated person(s) carries out the interventions that have been carefully selected and outlined in the Behavior Intervention Plan.

Again, the main purpose of conducting the functional assessment is to develop a Behavior Intervention Plan that includes positive interventions aimed at changing student behavior. The plans are not just developed and written into the Behavior Intervention Plan, but must be implemented appropriately with the student.

As noted earlier, teachers and other personnel responsible for implementing the Behavior Intervention Plan need to be provided training and support in the use of selected interventions if deemed necessary. To be effective, interventions must be implemented consistently and correctly. This is where an attempt is made, for instance, to work with the student by teaching a replacement or new behavior, modifying curriculum or instructional strategies, manipulating the antecedents or the consequences, or selecting other interventions that specifically address the problem behavior.

How Long Do I Implement the Interventions? The length of the interventions to be implemented will vary depending on the severity of the behavior, the frequency and intensity of the behavior, the type of intervention(s) used and their success with students. Another factor to consider when estimating the length of time required to implement an intervention is how effective and comfortable the teacher is in implementing the plan. The authors suggest that the intervention plan be reviewed at the end of 3 weeks to determine the amount of progress made by the student. However, the Behavior Intervention Plan can be reviewed and revised before the end of 3 weeks if deemed necessary by the team. For severe and complex behaviors, the process may require a more thorough and intense assessment process.

Step 9. Collect Behavioral Data

Once interventions are being implemented, the second phase of assessment begins. Data collection will be conducted during the intervention phase as outlined in step 3. When the selected interventions are in effect with the student, the classroom teacher begins the second phase of data collection--gathering intervention data. This includes observing and recording the behavior in the context or environment where it occurs. The data collection procedures used during the initial observation phase (baseline data) are also used to collect data during the intervention phase. This is done so that comparisons can be made with the baseline data to determine the effectiveness or ineffectiveness of the intervention(s) tried.

McConnell et al. (1998) suggest that the intervention data be collected regularly for at least 3 weeks during implementation of the Behavioral Intervention Plan. After week 3 at the follow-up team meeting, the intervention data will be compared to baseline data as discussed in step 10 to determine and evaluate the effectiveness of the proposed Behavior Intervention Plan. Behavior intervention data will continue to be collected as needed or per team decision.

Step 10. Conduct a Follow-up Team Meeting

During this step, the educational team meets to review and compare intervention data to baseline data and to discuss the student's behavior progress. As part of this step, intervention data are examined closely so a determination can be made regarding the success of the intervention plan. Did the interventions work? If the plan has demonstrated success in changing the student's behavior, it will be continued with modifications as needed. The team continues to monitor student progress and evaluate outcomes as needed. To be considered a successful intervention plan, the target behavior should decrease or be reduced at or near zero.

If the behavior intervention is not working, the team must examine why, starting by reviewing the hypothesis. In this effort, the following questions should be revisited and examined if necessary:

1. Were interventions carried out accurately and consistently as planned?
2. Is there some pertinent information lacking from the functional assessment?
3. Was the target behavior clearly identified and defined?
4. Were data collection methods accurate?
5. Did the team select and use multiple sources of data collection?
6. Did the teacher understand the interventions?
7. Did the student understand the interventions?

If necessary, a new hypothesis and a new plan are developed. Steps 6 through 10 are repeated for all Behavioral Intervention Plans that are determined to be unsuccessful.

A Functional Assessment Checklist (FAC) as shown in Figure 19 can be used by the functional assessment team to monitor the completion of the functional behavior assessment process. To be effective, each of the 10 steps described needs to be addressed. By following the 10 steps outlined in this publication and concurrently completing the appropriate forms, the task of working with students who demonstrate academic and behavioral problems becomes more systemic and consistent.

FUNCTIONAL ASSESSMENT CHECKLIST (FAC)

Student _____ Date of Birth _____ School _____

Date _____ Grade _____ Referred by _____

Reason for Referral _____

Facilitator _____ Date of Implementation _____

Review Dates _____ _____ _____ _____ _____ _____

Functional Assessment Procedures: (Check if applicable)   Date Completed/Initial:

1. ☐ Meet with classroom teacher(s) to identify and define target behavior   _____

2. ☐ Complete **TARGET BEHAVIOR ASSESSMENT FORM**   _____

3. ☐ Collect baseline data   _____

4. ☐ Complete **STUDENT INTERVIEW FORM**   _____

5. ☐ Gather information from parents   _____

6. ☐ Complete **MEDICAL FORM**   _____

7. ☐ Review academic information and assessment   _____

8. ☐ Review existing evaluation data   _____

9. ☐ Complete **EDUCATIONAL AND ENVIRONMENTAL ANALYSIS FORM**   _____

10. ☐ Review records   _____

11. ☐ Review discipline records   _____

12. ☐ Complete **BEHAVIOR INTERVENTION PLAN SHEET**   _____

13. ☐ Hold first team meeting   _____

14. ☐ Complete **FUNCTIONAL ASSESSMENT INTERVIEW FORM**   _____

15. ☐ Formulate hypothesis   _____

16. ☐ Write **BEHAVIOR INTERVENTION PLAN**   _____

17. ☐ Implement **BEHAVIOR INTERVENTION PLAN**   _____

18. ☐ Collect intervention data (3 weeks)   _____

19. ☐ Hold 3-week team meeting   _____

20. ☐ Schedule follow-up team meeting   _____

FIGURE 19. Functional Assessment Checklist (FAC).

CONCLUSION

The IDEA Amendments of 1997 require changes in the way we address the academic and behavior needs of students with disabilities. Specifically, local education agencies must conduct a functional assessment and implement a Behavioral Intervention Plan that includes positive behavioral supports for students with disabilities who have specific behavioral issues.

Assessing student behavior through the detailed process of functional assessment is crucial to the development of an effective Behavior Intervention Plan (Foster-Johnson & Dunlap, 1993). Functional assessment can be a valuable process for determining the cause(s) of a student's behavior and when writing Behavior Intervention Plans. When the functional assessment process as outlined in this book is followed and implemented, the result is the development of a Behavior Intervention Plan that includes effective behavior management strategies, interventions, and supports that in turn are beneficial to the student's school success.

In order to develop effective Behavior Intervention Plans, educators need knowledge about and training in functional assessment procedures. This manual has presented steps and procedures that educators can use when conducting functional assessments with students in school-based and other applicable settings. We hope that the information will guide educators in developing effective Behavior Intervention Plans for students with challenging behaviors based on the information derived from the functional assessment. We encourage school-based personnel to implement the procedures outlined in this manual and use the forms presented when conducting functional assessments in their schools.

REFERENCES

Bradley, D. F. & West, F. J. (1994). Staff training for the inclusion of students with disabilities: Visions from school-based educators. *Teacher Education and Special Education, 17*(2), 117–128.

Carr, E. G., & Durand, V. M. (1985). Reducing behavior problems through functional communication training. *Journal of Applied Behavior Analysis, 18,* 111–126.

Coleman, M. C. (1992). *Behavior disorders: Theory and practice.* Boston: Allyn & Bacon.

Dollard, N., Christen, L., Colucci, K., & Epanchin, B. (1996). Constructive classroom management. *Focus on Exceptional Children, 29*(2), 1–12.

Dunlap, G., Kern, L., dePerczel, M. Clark, S., Wilson, D., Childs, K. E., White, R., & Falk, G. D. (1993). Functional analysis of classroom variables for students with emotional and behavioral challenges. *Behavioral Disorders, 18,* 275–291.

Foster-Johnson, L., & Dunlap, G. (1993). Using functional assessment to develop effective, individualized interventions for challenging behavior. *Teaching Exceptional Children, 15*(3), 44–50.

Fuchs, D., & Fuchs, L. (1994). Inclusive schools movement and the radicalization of special education reform. *Exceptional Children, 60*(4), 294–309.

Gable, R. A., Quinn, M. M., Rutherford, R. B. & Howell, K. (1998). Addressing problem behaviors in schools: Assessments and Behavior Intervention Plans. *Preventing School Failure, 42*(3), 106–119.

Greenwood, C. R. Carta, J. J., Kamps, D., Terry, B., & Delquadri, J. (1994). Development and validation of standard classroom observation systems for school practitioners: Ecobehavioral assessment systems software (EBASS). *Exceptional Children, 61*(2), 197–210.

Hallahan, D., & Kauffman, J. (1994). *Exceptional Children.* Boston: Allyn & Bacon.

Haynes, S. N. (1998). The changing nature of behavioral assessment. In A. S. Bellack & M. Hersen (Eds.), *Behavioral assessment: A practical handbook.* Boston: Allyn & Bacon.

Horner, R. H., O'Neil, R. E., & Flannery, K. B. (1993). Building effective behavior support plans from functional assessment information. In M. Snell (Ed), *Instruction of Persons With Severe Handicaps* (4th ed. pp. 184–214). Columbus, OH: Merrill.

Johns, B. H. (1998). What the new individuals with disabilities education act (IDEA) means for students who exhibit aggressive or violent behavior. *Preventing School Failure, 42*(3), 102–105.

Johns, B. H. & Carr, V. G. (1995). *Techniques for managing verbally and physically aggressive students.* Denver, Love Publishing.

IDEA Amendments of 1997, 20 U.S.C. 1400 *et seq.*

Individuals with Disabilities Education Act of 1990, 20 U.S.C. 1400 *et seq.*

Kaplan, J. S., & Carter, J. (1995). *Beyond behavior modification.* Austin, Texas: PRO-ED, Inc.

Kauffman, J., M. & Wong, K., L., H. (1991). Effective teachers of students with behavioral disorders: Are generic teaching skills enough? *Behavioral Disorders, 16*(3), 71–78.

Kerr, M. M. & Nelson, C. M. (1983). *Strategies for managing behavior problems in the classroom.* Columbus, OH: Merrill/Macmillan.

Kerr, M. M., & Nelson, C. M. (1998). *Strategies for managing behavior problems in the Classroom.* Upper Saddle River, New Jersey: Prentice-Hall.

MacAuley, D. J. & Johnson, G. M. (1993). Behaviorally disordered students in mainstream settings: A pedagogical-interactional perspective. *Teacher Education Quarterly, 20*(3), 87–100.

McConnell, M. E., Hilvitz, P. B., & C. J. Cox (1998). Functional Assessment: A systematic process for assessment and intervention in general and special education classrooms. *Intervention in School and Clinic, 34*(1), 10–20.

Meese, R. L. (1994). *Teaching learners with mild disabilities: Integrating research and practice.* Pacific Grove, CA.: Brooks/Cole Publishing Company.

Miller, J. A., Tansy, M., & Hughes, T. L. (1998). Functional behavioral assessment: The link between problem behavior and effective intervention in schools. *Current Issues in Education, 1*(1), 1–16.

O'Neil, R. E., Horner, R. H., Albin, R. W., Storey, K., & Sprague, J. R. (1990). *Functional analysis and program behavior: A practical assessment guide.* Sycamore, IL: Sycamore.

Quinn, M. M., Gable, R. A., Rutherford, R. B., Nelson, C. M., & Howell, K. W. (1998). Addressing student problem behavior: *An IEP team's Introduction to functional behavioral assessment and behavior intervention plans* (2nd ed.). Washington, DC: The Center for Effective Collaboration and Practice.

Ruhl, K. L. & Berlinghoff, D. H. (1992). Research on improving behaviorally disordered students' academic performance: A review of the literature. *Behavioral Disorders, 17*(3), 178–190.

Shaw, S. R., & Swerdik, M. R. (1995). Best practices facilitating team functioning. In A. Thomas & J. Grimes (Eds.), *Best Practices in School Psychology* (3rd ed., pp. 153–159). Washington, DC: National Association of School Psychologists.

Yell, M., & Shriner, J. (1997). The IDEA amendments of 1997: Implications for special and general education teachers, administrators, and teacher trainers. *Focus on Exceptional Children, 30*(1), 1–20.

Zaragoza, N., Vaughn, S., & McIntosh, R. (1991). Social skills interventions and children with behavior problems: A review. *Behavioral Disorders, 16*(4), 260–275.

APPENDIX A

TARGET BEHAVIOR
ASSESSMENT FORM

TARGET BEHAVIOR ASSESSMENT FORM

Teacher _____ Student _____ Date _____

List problem behaviors exhibited by student:

_____

_____

_____

Write a detailed description of one problem behavior:

_____

_____

_____

_____

Describe the physical environment where the behavior occurs:

_____

_____

_____

List the instructional expectations of the class in which the behavior occurs:

_____

_____

_____

List the behavioral expectations of the class in which the behavior occurs:

_____

_____

_____

Attach and bring to the team meeting:

1. Records of behavior occurrences (frequency/duration counts).
2. Academic work information and work samples showing the student's academic ability in reading (rate and comprehension), math computation, and written language.

APPENDIX B

DATA COLLECTION FORMS

ANECDOTAL RECORDING FORM

Student:_____   Class:_____   Activity:_____

School:_____   Teacher:_____   Date:_____

Grade:_____

Time   Behavior Observed

Time   Behavior Observed

Time   Behavior Observed

FREQUENCY COUNT RECORDING

Student_____ Behavior_____

Observer_____ Class_____

Mark each time the behavior occurs.   Baseline_____ Intervention_____

Date	Time Observed	Frequency Count

Comments:

DURATION AND A-B-C OBSERVATION FORM

Baseline _____

Student _____

Behavior _____

Observer _____

Intervention _____

Date	Time	Length of Behavior	What Occurred Prior to the Behavior	Describe Behavior	Outcome of Behavior

INTERVAL AND TIME SAMPLING OBSERVATION SHEET

Teacher_____Student_____Grade_____

Observer_____Time started _____Time ended _____

Behavior _____Activity_____Date _____

Recording Codes: + = Occurrence
                  o = Nonoccurrence

Baseline_____ Intervention _____

Observation Intervals: 10   20   30
                              (seconds)

APPENDIX C

GRAPHING FORMS

SELF-GRAPHING SHEET

NAME: _____ BEHAVIOR: _____

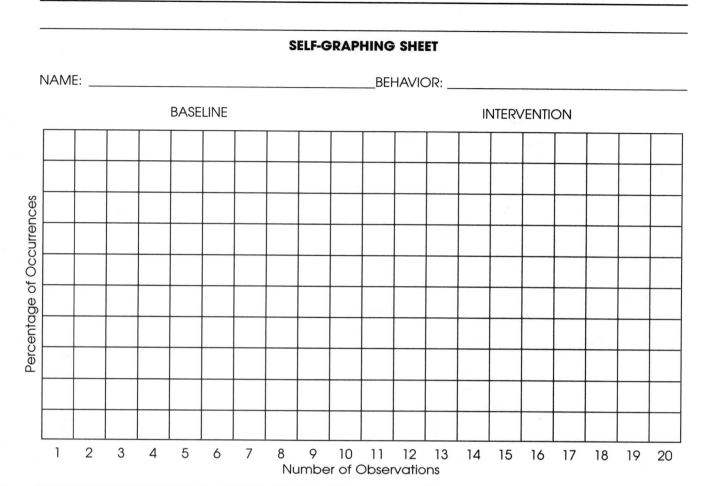

BASELINE   INTERVENTION

SELF-GRAPHING SHEET

NAME: _____ BEHAVIOR: _____

Beginning Date: _____ Ending Date: _____

BASELINE   INTERVENTION(S)

NUMBER OF OCCURRENCES

| | 1 | 2 | 3 | 4 | 5 | 6 | 7 | 8 | 9 | 10 | 11 | 12 | 13 | 14 | 15 | 16 | 17 | 18 | 19 | 20 |

OBSERVATION DAYS

BEHAVIOR OBSERVATION GRAPHING SHEET

Name: _____ Behavior: _____

Circle the number of times the behavior occurs for each date.
Connect circles to form graph.

BASELINE ——— INTERVENTION(S) – – – – –

	1	2	3	4	5	6	7	8	9	10	11	12	13	14	15	16	17	18
20	20	20	20	20	20	20	20	20	20	20	20	20	20	20	20	20	20	20
19	19	19	19	19	19	19	19	19	19	19	19	19	19	19	19	19	19	19
18	18	18	18	18	18	18	18	18	18	18	18	18	18	18	18	18	18	18
17	17	17	17	17	17	17	17	17	17	17	17	17	17	17	17	17	17	17
16	16	16	16	16	16	16	16	16	16	16	16	16	16	16	16	16	16	16
15	15	15	15	15	15	15	15	15	15	15	15	15	15	15	15	15	15	15
14	14	14	14	14	14	14	14	14	14	14	14	14	14	14	14	14	14	14
13	13	13	13	13	13	13	13	13	13	13	13	13	13	13	13	13	13	13
12	12	12	12	12	12	12	12	12	12	12	12	12	12	12	12	12	12	12
11	11	11	11	11	11	11	11	11	11	11	11	11	11	11	11	11	11	11
10	10	10	10	10	10	10	10	10	10	10	10	10	10	10	10	10	10	10
9	9	9	9	9	9	9	9	9	9	9	9	9	9	9	9	9	9	9
8	8	8	8	8	8	8	8	8	8	8	8	8	8	8	8	8	8	8
7	7	7	7	7	7	7	7	7	7	7	7	7	7	7	7	7	7	7
6	6	6	6	6	6	6	6	6	6	6	6	6	6	6	6	6	6	6
5	5	5	5	5	5	5	5	5	5	5	5	5	5	5	5	5	5	5
4	4	4	4	4	4	4	4	4	4	4	4	4	4	4	4	4	4	4
3	3	3	3	3	3	3	3	3	3	3	3	3	3	3	3	3	3	3
2	2	2	2	2	2	2	2	2	2	2	2	2	2	2	2	2	2	2
1	1	1	1	1	1	1	1	1	1	1	1	1	1	1	1	1	1	1
	1	2	3	4	5	6	7	8	9	10	11	12	13	14	15	16	17	18

Observation Days

Intervention(s): _____

Appendix D

Student Interview Form

STUDENT INTERVIEW FORM

Name: _____   Date: _____

Interviewer:_____   Class: _____

Complete with student.

1. What things do you generally do that gets you in trouble at school?

   _____

   _____

   _____

2. What are you doing when the behavior occurs and what usually happens afterwards?

   _____

   _____

   _____

3. When and where do the behaviors generally occur?

   _____

   _____

   _____

4. How would you describe your behavior at school?

   _____

   _____

   _____

5. What do you do when you get angry?

   _____

6. What do you like most about school?

   _____

   _____

   _____

7. What things do you not like to do at school?

_____

_____

_____

8. What teacher behavior especially bothers you?

_____

_____

_____

9. What are your favorite classes?

_____

_____

10. What classes are hard for you?

_____

_____

11. What can your teachers do to help you be more successful at school?

_____

_____

_____

_____

12. List some things you do best:

_____

_____

_____

Additional Comments:

_____

_____

_____

_____

_____

Appendix E

Medical Information Form

MEDICAL ASSESSMENT FORM

Name _____ Date _____ Grade _____

School _____ D.O.B. _____ Age _____

Person(s) completing form _____

Date of Last Physical Examination: _____

Vision Results: _____

_____

Hearing Results: _____

_____

1. Medical diagnosis (if any):

2. Does the medical diagnosis have an effect on the student's behavior?

3. Is the student on medication?

4. What type?

5. Are there side effects to the medication? Describe.

6. Are there questions about the side effects?

7. How and with whom is the medication administered?

Appendix F

Educational and Environmental Analysis

EDUCATIONAL AND ENVIRONMENTAL ANALYSIS

Teacher:

Course Subject:

Grade:

Type of Classroom:

School:

Classroom Location:

Length of Class:

No. of Students in Class:

Interviewer:

Date:

1. CLASSROOM ENVIRONMENT

Describe your classroom set-up and student seating arrangement:

Identify distractors:

2. CLASSROOM MANAGEMENT

What are the classroom rules?

What are the consequences for breaking classroom rules?

How do you handle student conflicts and/or discipline issues?

3. INSTRUCTIONAL DELIVERY

What instructional methods do you use?

What does a class period generally consist of?

Are students given free time during your class period? If so, how much and what activities do they engage In?

How do you work with students in your classroom?

4. COURSE REQUIREMENTS

What are students required to do in your class?

What materials and supplies are needed by students?

How much class participation is required by students?

What skills do students need to be successful in your classroom?

5. CLASS ASSIGNMENTS
What types of assignments are given?

Describe frequency of assignments:

How are directions presented?

What are your homework requirements?

6. INSTRUCTIONAL MATERIALS
Title of textbook used:

What supplemental instructional materials are used?

What modifications are made for students with disabilities?

7. GRADING SYSTEM
What kinds of tests are given?

How often?

What is your make-up policy for assignments, homework, and tests?

Describe your grading criteria:

8. TEACHER BEHAVIORS
What do you like about your class?

What do you like about the curriculum you teach?

Is there anything you would change about the way you conduct your class?

Appendix G

Functional Assessment Interview Form

FUNCTIONAL ASSESSMENT INTERVIEW FORM

Student _____   Teacher _____

Team Member's Name   Team Member's Position

_____   _____

_____   _____

_____   _____

_____   _____

A. Describe the Behavior:

    1. What is the behavior?

    2. How is the behavior performed?

    3. How often does the behavior occur?

    4. How long does the behavior last when it occurs?

    5. What is the intensity of the behavior when it occurs?

B. Define Setting Events and Environmental Factors That Predict the Behavior (describe the following variables):

    1. Classroom structure (physical).

    2. Class rules and procedural expectations.

    3. Instructional delivery (lecture, cooperative learning, labs, etc.).

    4. Instructional materials (textbooks, worksheets, hands-on activities).

    5. How are directions presented?

    6. Assessment techniques (multiple-choice tests, essay tests, rubrics, authentic assessment).

C. Define Specific Immediate Antecedent Events That Predict When the Behaviors Are Most Likely to Occur:

1. When are the behaviors most likely to occur?

2. When are the behaviors least likely to occur?

3. Where are the behaviors most likely to occur?

4. Where are the behaviors least likely to occur?

5. During what activities are the behaviors most likely to occur?

6. During what activities are the behaviors least likely to occur?

D. Identify Specific Consequences That Follow the Behavior:

1. What specific consequence is most likely to immediately follow the behavior?

2. What seems to be the effect of the consequence on the student's behavior?

3. Does the consequence remove the student from an uncomfortable situation?

4. Is there consistency between the consequences given by the classroom teacher and the consequences given by the administrators?

5. Is there consistent follow-through with all consequences both in the classroom and in the school office?

APPENDIX H

BEHAVIORAL INTERVENTION PLAN SHEET

BEHAVIORAL INTERVENTION PLAN SHEET

Please complete this form and bring to the team meeting.

Student _____   Teacher _____   Date _____

Disability _____   School _____   Grade _____

1. Describe behavioral issues.

   _____
   _____
   _____
   _____

2. What disciplinary actions has the student received for inappropriate behavior?

   _____
   _____
   _____
   _____

3. How does the student respond to adults?

   _____
   _____
   _____
   _____

4. What interventions/strategies have you tried?

   _____
   _____
   _____
   _____

5. How were they implemented?

   _____
   _____
   _____

6. How long were they implemented?

_____

_____

_____

_____

_____

7. Which interventions were effective?

_____

_____

_____

_____

_____

8. Which interventions were not effective?

_____

_____

_____

_____

_____

9. What are you currently doing?

_____

_____

_____

_____

_____

10. What would you like to try?

_____

_____

_____

_____

_____

APPENDIX I

BEHAVIOR INTERVENTION PLAN

BEHAVIOR INTERVENTION PLAN (BIP)

Student: _____   School: _____

Date Developed: _____   Date Implemented: _____

Grade _____

Baseline Data Results:

Hypothesis Statement:

Type of Intervention Plan: Educational _____   Behavioral _____

Person(s) Responsible for Implementing Plan:

DESCRIPTION OF THE BEHAVIOR:

BEHAVIOR   BEHAVIOR DEFINED

INTERVENTION GOAL:

INTERVENTION PLAN:

1.

2.

3.

4.

5.

WHEN AND WHERE THE PLAN WILL BE IMPLEMENTED:

INTERVENTION DATA COLLECTION SUMMARY:

Week 1

Week 2

Week 3

FOLLOW-UP AND REVIEW DATE(S):

COMMENTS:

TEAM MEETING PARTICIPANTS:

Name	Position
_____	_____
_____	_____
_____	_____
_____	_____
_____	_____

APPENDIX J

FUNCTIONAL ASSESSMENT CHECKLIST (FAC)

FUNCTIONAL ASSESSMENT CHECKLIST (FAC)

Student _____ Date of Birth _____ School _____

Date _____ Grade _____ Referred by _____

Reason for Referral _____

Facilitator _____ Date of Implementation _____

Review Dates _____   _____   _____   _____   _____   _____

Functional Assessment Procedures: (Check if applicable)   Date Completed/Initial:

1. ☐ Meet with classroom teacher(s) to identify and define target behavior   _____

2. ☐ Complete **TARGET BEHAVIOR ASSESSMENT FORM**   _____

3. ☐ Collect baseline data   _____

4. ☐ Complete **STUDENT INTERVIEW FORM**   _____

5. ☐ Gather information from parents   _____

6. ☐ Complete **MEDICAL FORM**   _____

7. ☐ Review academic information and assessment   _____

8. ☐ Review existing evaluation data   _____

9. ☐ Complete **EDUCATIONAL AND ENVIRONMENTAL ANALYSIS FORM**   _____

10. ☐ Review records   _____

11. ☐ Review discipline records   _____

12. ☐ Complete **BEHAVIOR INTERVENTION PLAN SHEET**   _____

13. ☐ Hold first team meeting   _____

14. ☐ Complete **FUNCTIONAL ASSESSMENT INTERVIEW FORM**   _____

15. ☐ Formulate hypothesis   _____

16. ☐ Write **BEHAVIOR INTERVENTION PLAN**   _____

17. ☐ Implement **BEHAVIOR INTERVENTION PLAN**   _____

18. ☐ Collect intervention data (3 weeks)   _____

19. ☐ Hold three-week team meeting   _____

20. ☐ Schedule follow-up team meeting   _____

INDEX